God's Not Broke

How I Discovered 21 Laws of Prosperity

Paul Pimentel

God's Not Broke: How I Discovered 21 Laws of Prosperity
Copyright © 2014 by Paul Pimentel

ISBN 978-0-692-40572-7

Printed in the USA by the Pimentel Press.

Dedication

What an amazing God we serve. I want to thank the Lord for an opportunity to minister His Word, and I also want to thank Him for not being a man who lies (**Numbers 23:19**). His Word is true. I give Him praise for using me and for the visions He has given me – visions that have and continue to come to pass. What an amazing ride! Lord, I, your servant, love you.

I also want to dedicate this book to my family. Over 25 years ago, you "left all" to do God's perfect will.

Lori, thank you for being with me 42 years, for hearing God and for agreeing to come along for the journey. Not only did you support me in becoming a pioneer pastor, but you also stood by my side to build a business, Pimentel Communications Inc. Without you, this wouldn't be possible; none of it could have been done. God gave me the perfect wife.

With all my love,
Your Hubby

Lorinda, Paulie and David: I love all of you so much. Thank you for your sacrifice. Thank you for leaving your home, grandparents, uncles, aunts, cousins and friends for a new, unfamiliar land. It was a land where we knew nobody but God. It was the land to where God led us. I'm so proud of each of you and enjoy watching what God is doing in your lives. It's amazing!

- Dad

Endorsements

"Paul Pimentel is an amazing example, as both a recipient and a conduit, of God's generosity. To me, he has been a great friend and an amazingly helpful ministry supporter. Nobody I know personally is sowing more financial seeds into the great harvest of souls. His story will inspire you to think bigger, challenge you to do more and, ultimately, connect you with God's power to prosper. I am happy to recommend *God's Not Broke*. If you want to understand and live in God's prosperity, this is the book for you."

~ David Diga Hernandez
Evangelist, Author and TV Host
David Hernandez Ministries

"As a friend of Paul Pimentel, I can say with certainty that this man lives what he preaches. His life constantly inspires those around him to speak life and faith into even the toughest of circumstances. Paul went from being an impoverished fruit picker to becoming a pastor and millionaire businessman, who sows into the Kingdom. His amazing testimony stands as a unique declaration that God's Word is true. Paul has lived what he teaches you in this book. His story demonstrates that the Biblical laws of prosperity work, and they can work for you too."

~ Kelly Lohrke
Pastor and Author
Praise Chapel Kansas City

"God's Not Broke by Paul Pimentel is a unique read that allows you to see a man's journey from poverty to wealth, while also discovering his destiny. His transparent nature not only shows the struggles he went through but also God's faithfulness that delivers and leads a man to God's promised land. If you desire to learn to trust God with your life, with your finances and desire to be a person that builds the Kingdom, the principles shared in *God's Not Broke* will help change your life. It will also help you establish a plan for kingdom prosperity!"

~ Rob Sanchez
Prophet and Author
Prophetic Firstfruits Int. Ministries

Table of Contents

Introduction

The prosperity of Heaven reaches beyond your bank account. It is not bound to the confines of your wallet. When I write of prosperity, I am writing of something more than monetary gain. Prosperity is more than having money in both your saving and checking accounts. God wants you to prosper in your relationships, your business, your ministry and your home. God wants to bless your life, and His concern touches every aspect of it.

**"The Lord directs the steps of the godly.
He delights in every detail of their lives."**
~ Psalm 37:23

Heaven is a kingdom, and every kingdom has a culture. What is the culture of God's realm? What is the taste of the Father? When your realm looks like God's realm – that's prosperity. When you think like God thinks, talk like God talks and act like God acts – that's prosperity. God is generous. God is grand. God is dramatic. We must assimilate to the Heavenly realm. After all, it is our home.

We must see prosperity for what it is: Heaven's culture in our lives.

Though this idea of prosperity should be fundamental in the life of every believer, it is often rejected as vice. With a sort of pious approach to prosperity, most believers think of it to be invasive or even a barrier to spirituality.

"Prosperity" is perceived as a dirty word. This perception goes beyond even church culture. Now days, successful businessmen are portrayed as the villains. Anyone who has influence is "the man" against whom rebellion is encouraged.

The reality: Poverty is not a requirement of salvation. Negativity is not a result of a renewed mind. And small thinking is not humble. Heaven is not a welfare state. You serve a big God, able to do above and beyond what you can imagine.

We are kings and priests. Priests steward the spiritual. Kings steward the earthly. When a man lives in prosperity, he is positioned, in every regard, to be a prime and efficient sower of gospel seed. His wallet preaches the gospel. His family's peace preaches the gospel. His orderly life preaches the gospel. His work ethic preaches the gospel. God wants us to have order in our homes, influence in our words and finance in our hands. And it is the preaching of the gospel that must be our highest priority.

The gospel is free, but the means to deliver it is pricy. For the most part, people no longer gather on grassy hills for social interaction, and they are much more distracted than ever before. In society today, the message must be delivered to where the people are. We must permeate the culture with the gospel – television, venues, radio, internet, media, books and platforms of all sorts. We must get the gospel into the systems of education, entertainment, government and business.

And prosperity is the most ideal position from which we can most effectively declare the truth of the gospel. Martin Luther put it this way:

"There is nothing that Satan can bear less than the light of the Gospel. When it shines, he becomes furious and tries with all his might to extinguish it. He attempts this in two ways: first, by the deceit of heretics and the might of tyrants; secondly, by poverty and famine. Because Satan has been unable thus far to suppress the Gospel in our territories through heretics and tyrants, he is now trying the second way; he is depriving the ministers of the Word of their livelihood, so that poverty and famine will force them to forsake their ministry, and the unfortunate people, deprived of the Word, will eventually degenerate into animals."

In every war, there must be supply. And some are called to be Kingdom suppliers. Is that you? Then it's time for change. It's time to move beyond frustration and into the culture of Heaven.

You're not called to be powerless. You're not called to be broke. If it so burns in your heart, it can manifest in your hand. What joy it will be when you become one who meets the needs of the Kingdom. What ecstasy it is to carry and distribute the resources of Heaven. That can be you.

You may say, "Paul, I can hardly pay my own bills, but I want to begin to fund the Kingdom." I assure you of this: if you will obey God's Word, you can walk in prosperity. The key is to overcome ignorance and disobedience. To do so, you must know what God's Word teaches on these matters.

So what does the Word say concerning these matters? Before you delve into my story, I want you to consider this question: is poverty godly?

If poverty is a godly trait, nobody told that to Abraham, Isaac, Jacob, King David, King Solomon or even Joseph of Arimathea, who was a disciple of Christ. You may have been told that, in order to be a true disciple of Christ, you must be poor or despise wealth. But the good news is that's not the Biblical truth.

"As evening approached, there came a rich man from Arimathea, named Joseph, who had himself become a disciple of Jesus."
~ Matthew 27:57

But I thought that riches keep you from surrendering to God! Yes, they can. But Joseph (and the various rich godly men in scripture) are examples of people who were not kept away from truly godly lives because of riches. It is safe to conclude that godliness and prosperity are not at odds with one another, unless you allow them to be. This is true of anything else, though money is especially seductive.

A more balanced approach would be found in proverbs.

"First, help me never to tell a lie. Second, give me neither poverty nor riches! Give me just enough to satisfy my needs."
~ Proverbs 30:8

Keep this in mind: that verse was written by one of the wealthiest, wisest men who ever lived. Believe me, he did not give up his riches. But he is teaching us the wisdom of contentment. Wealth, though not evil to have, can become an evil, consuming pursuit.

"But people who long to be rich fall into temptation and are trapped by many foolish and harmful desires that plunge them into ruin and destruction. For the love of money is the root of all kinds of evil. And some people, craving money, have wandered from the true faith and pierced themselves with many sorrows."

~ 1 Timothy 6:9 – 10

It is the longing for riches, the love of money, that brings about great temptation. In short, you can have riches as long as riches don't have you. In fact, just below the famous scripture, we find the context to be more nuanced than some would have you believe.

"...each those who are rich in this world not to be proud and not to trust in their money, which is so unreliable. Their trust should be in God, who richly gives us all we need for our enjoyment. Tell them to use their money to do good. They should be rich in good works and generous to those in need, always being ready to share with others. By doing this they will be storing up their treasure as a good foundation for the future so that they may experience true life."

~ 1 Timothy 6:17-19

The scripture does not tell those who are rich to give up their riches. It tells them to use their riches *for godliness.* In fact, those who are rich can use their riches to store up for themselves spiritual treasure.

Also, note that God not only provides everything we need for living, but He provides everything that we need for enjoyment: "...**who richly gives us all we need for our enjoyment...**" The implication here is that God actually was the one who provided the riches.

13

I believe in sacrifice. I believe in carrying your cross. But often we, as those of times past, whip ourselves in an effort to pay a price that has already been paid. Give up riches for the gospel? Yes. Continue to generate riches to spread the gospel? Yes to that too.

The issue is the heart. It's always been the heart. The rich young ruler, the rich man in Hell and the rich people who would be harder to fit into Heaven than a camel into the eye of a needle – it is always about their hearts.

We must not, as the Pharisees did, compile our own religious rules to burden people. We often make it harder for people to enter the Kingdom of Heaven than it already is.

For righteousness, poverty and prosperity are neutral – God looks at the heart. It's what one does in such predicaments that makes a man godly. Has God called some to live in difficult terrain to fulfill their ministry tasks? Yes. But He has also called some to generate finances for the sake of the gospel. Don't lose that perspective.

Poverty, though unfortunately sometimes championed, is taught by scripture to be a result of poor choices, whether direct or indirect. Keep in mind that this is not a blanket generalization.

"Lazy hands make for poverty, but diligent hands bring wealth."
~ Proverbs 10:4

Which do you think the scripture is condoning in that verse? Hard work or laziness? Of course, we know that the scripture teaches us to work hard. So the truth is that there is a positive light shed on wealth by scripture.

"The blessing of the LORD makes a person rich, and he adds no sorrow with it."
~ Proverbs 10:22

Here again we see that wealth comes from the Lord.

But doesn't Jesus condemn wealth?

Yes, He does, but only when that wealth keeps you from godliness. There are two ways to look at wealth. Wealth can either be a tool for the Kingdom or a barrier to it. This is the key verse.

"I know what it is to be in need, and I know what it is to have plenty. I have learned the secret of being content in any and every situation, whether well fed or hungry, whether living in plenty or in want."

~ Philippians 4:12

Poverty is not itself godly. And prosperity (plenty) can be good. Is it wrong to ask God for wealth? No! Is it wrong for that desire to become a longing? Yes. Just keep your heart right.

Poverty, though we sometimes may face it, is never generally or absolutely necessary for the spreading of the gospel, though it may be encountered from time to time. But lack is not to be embraced. God wants to supply you with all that you need to fulfill your mission, and you mustn't feel guilty to ask for such a supply.

Poverty causes hunger. Is hunger godly? Poverty causes disease. Is disease godly? Poverty causes lack. Is lack godly? If so, why is Heaven so Heavenly? If that were the case, why wouldn't our eternal reward be that of lack, disease or hunger? That's because poverty is not the culture of Heaven. It is not God's desire for His children.

Here are a few key verses upon which I want you to meditate:

"Trust in the Lord, and do good; so shalt thou dwell in the land, and verily thou shalt be fed. Delight thyself also in the Lord: and he shall give thee the desires of thine heart. Commit thy way unto the Lord; trust also in him; and he shall bring it to pass. But the meek shall inherit the earth; and shall delight themselves in the abundance of peace."

~ Psalm 37:3-5,11

"I have been young, and now am old; yet have I not seen the righteous forsaken, or his seed begging bread. He is ever merciful, and lendeth; and his seed is blessed."

~ Psalm 37:25-26*

*The context indicates material blessing.

"For the Lord God is a sun and shield: the Lord will give grace and glory: no good thing will he withhold from them that walk uprightly"

~ Psalm 84:11-12

"Yea, the Lord shall give that which is good; and our land shall yield her increase."

~ Psalm 85:12

"Therefore take no thought, saying, What shall we eat? or, What shall we drink: or, wherewithal shall we be clothed? (For after all these things do the Gentiles seek:) for your heavenly Father knoweth that ye have need of all these things. But seek ye first the kingdom of God, and his righteousness; and all these things shall be added unto you."

~ Matthew 6:31-33

"Nevertheless he left not himself without witness, in that he did good, and gave us rain from heaven, and fruitful season, filling our hearts with food and gladness."

~ Acts 14:17

"Honor thy Lord with thy substance, and with the firstfruits of all thine increase: So shall thy barns be filled with plenty, and thy presses shall burst out with new wine."

~ Proverbs 3:9-10

"Riches and honour are with me: yea, durable riches and righteousness. My fruit is better than gold, yea, than fine gold; and my revenue than choice silver. I lead in the way of righteousness, in the midst of the paths of judgment; That I may cause those that love me to inherit substance; and I will fill their treasures."

~ Proverbs 8:18-21

"And my God will meet all your needs according to his glorious riches by the Anointed Jesus."

~ Philippians 4:19

"Yours, O Lord, is the greatness and the power and the glory and the majesty and the splendor, for everything in heaven and earth is yours. Yours, O Lord, is the kingdom; you are exalted as head over all. Wealth and honor come from you; you are the ruler of all things. In your hands are strength and power to exalt and give strength to all."

~ 1 Chronicles 29:11-12

"As for every man to whom God has given riches and wealth, and given him power to eat of it, to receive his heritage and rejoice in his labor—this is the gift of God."

~ Ecclesiastes 5:19

"Treasures of wickedness profit nothing, But righteousness delivers from death. The LORD will not allow the righteous soul to famish,But He casts away the desire of the wicked. He who has a slack hand becomes poor, But the hand of the diligent makes rich. He who gathers in summer is a wise son; He who sleeps in harvest is a son who causes shame. Blessings are on the head of the righteous, But violence covers the mouth of the wicked."

~ Proverbs 10:2-6

"The generous soul will be made rich, And he who waters will also be watered himself."

~ Proverbs 11:25

"But this I say: He who sows sparingly will also reap sparingly, and he who sows bountifully will also reap bountifully. So let each one give as he purposes in his heart, not grudgingly or of necessity; for God loves a cheerful giver."

~ 2 Corinthians 9:6-7

"What the righteous desire will be granted."

~Proverbs 10:24

So now that we know what the scripture teaches concerning prosperity, let us courageously embark on this journey of adventurous faith, the path to prosperity.

As you read through my story, you'll be given the 21 laws of prosperity that I consider to be most essential. The laws will be inserted along my chronicle, but they can also be read independently. Some sections of these laws are shorter than others, but the truths within each one of them can be immediately applied to your life.

Chapter 1
The Wolf

The wolf was born on March 13th 1955. I refer to my old self as "the wolf". As you'll soon learn, the wolf was not pleasant. Daily, I still have to die to the wolf. The wolf bites. The wolf growls. The wolf is vicious, intimidating. Though the wolf has been tamed to a balance of subdued harshness and channeled cunning, the wolf must yield to the Spirit.

Let me tell you about the wolf.

Soon after I was born, I began to learn both the pain and pleasure of hard work. At the age of 4, I could be found picking cotton out of a field. Like my father, I was a hard worker.

My father, a man's man, was strict and orderly. He taught me the value of hard work. Early mornings, hot days and exhausted nights – that was my life. But in spite of all of our hard work, we knew only the frustration of poverty – tiresome and restrictive poverty. We were dirt poor.

Now I believe that every culture has both its generational curses and blessings. Depending upon who they serve, a family will either reap the curse or the blessing. And that curse or blessing is primarily determined by the men of the family. So, growing up in an ungodly family, I lived under a curse.

I don't mean to make a generalization, but I am of Hispanic descent. Because my family was not serving God, I knew the negative aspects, the curses of that culture. The men in my family placed a strong emphasis on machismo, held a degrading perspective of women and drank. We drank *heavily*. I was, at first, an unfortunate witness to all of this. But, eventually, I became an un-reluctant participant.

From childhood to adolescence, I existed in an environment of sin. So my life was mundane. However, I caught a glimpse of my first ray of sunshine during my high school years. And that little ray of sunshine had a name.

#1 The Law of Work

But before I go further with my story, I thought that this would be a proper place to introduce to you the first law of prosperity, the law of hard work. Mind you, I didn't get saved until later in life, but the laws of prosperity work in even secular contexts. The laws of prosperity are so powerful that they often even work for non-believers. In fact, most of the fundamental principles that guide some of the largest and most successful businesses in the world find their roots in the truth of scripture. And this law is no different.

A very strong work ethic permanently marked me when I was very young.

I have found that, as far as true prosperity goes, there is no substitute or magic formula that can help you to bypass hard work. Many people, including believers, search for shortcuts and quick fixes. But the truth is that supposed quick fixes never get the job done right and later come to be regretted. You'll waste time doing patch-up work. Nothing will slow you down like a "quick fix".

Think about it this way. Prosperous people spend years working very hard, and, even with all of their incredibly ardent efforts, struggle to overcome the boundaries of their circumstances. Even with their hard work there is a great difficulty in ascending the hill. So what would make anyone believe that they can just coast at ease and float into the blessings of prosperity? You can't float into prosperity; you have to dig into prosperity. If obtaining prosperity is challenging for hard workers, how do the lazy expect to just stumble into success?

Prosperity is no accident. Prosperity is always on purpose. The scripture weighs in heavily on this issue:

"Lazy people want much but get little, but those who work hard will prosper."
~ Proverbs 13:4

Some will tell themselves that they are unwilling victims of their circumstance, that they can do nothing about their predicament. While it's true that some things are out of your control, you need to be honest with yourself. What is actually out of your control? Are you really looking for a way out? Or are you searching for anything that sounds like a legitimate excuse from hard work? Do you tell yourself that you can do nothing about it because you're too lazy to try? What is in your control? Work to better what you can better.

Even Christians milk the system, front feeble excuses and avoid burdens of responsibility. But we should be the hardest working people on earth, for we are given the greatest motivation of all.

"Work willingly at whatever you do, as though you were working for the Lord rather than for people."

~ Colossians 3:23

I'm an honest man, and I say what needs to be said, even when people don't necessarily want to hear it. So here it is: if you're lazy, you will never prosper. I don't write that to tear you down. I write it to wake you up.

How much time are we wasting on leisure that we tell ourselves that we deserve? Yes, I believe in rest, as you'll read in a later chapter of this book. But when was the last time that you, with shrewd honesty, evaluated your own work ethic? Have you accounted for the time you spend? How much television do you watch? And what's the quality of work that you deliver?

I know. That's intense!

Anything of high value will cost you much. The same is true of prosperity. Commit to hard work, and it will reward you.

So what if you're a hard worker and you still aren't seeing the results that you want to see?

The laws of prosperity work best when they're all being observed. Prosperity is like flight, and you are like an airplane. Thousands of intricate, complex functions have to go right before there can be flight. And, even if the majority of your engine's functions are working properly, if one important function is off, you won't be able to take off. So take a mental note, commit to hard work and let's continue.

The Law of Work: Prosperity is on purpose.

So now what of that ray of sunshine in my life?

The year was 1972. That was the year I met Lori Gabele. Tall, white and blonde, Lori grabbed my attention. It was soon after meeting Lori – June 29th – that her and I began to "go steady". And, just a few years later, we were married on July 30th 1977.

Our marriage was good, with only a few challenges here and there. I held a steady job at GTE, while Lori worked for her father's dental practice, David Gabele DDS. All things seemed to be in order.

But, deep within me, there were issues that I didn't even know I had. My childhood environment had imparted seeds within my soul, and I was soon approaching the time of dark harvest.

The wolf was waiting to attack.

About a year after being married, Lori and I had our first child. My daughter, Lorinda, was born on June 10th 1978.

Soon after Lorinda was born, I began to realize something: I didn't know how to share my wife. Maybe it was because of my insecurity. I recall being told by my family, during my childhood, that I was "ugly". Maybe it was because of my possessive womanizing. I learned that from watching the men in my family. Or perhaps it was because of the shame I felt from growing up poor. Whatever the reason, I took Lori's reduced attention on me as rejection. I just didn't know how to share my wife.

I'm not quite sure if that's what drove me to drinking. I suspect that my unaddressed issues had surfaced as a result of being shook by major life adjustments. Maybe it was the pressure of all that change. But I began to drink more.

I continued to work hard. I also continued to drink. Though I do not wish to glorify such chains, I must say that, when I drank, I became who I wanted to be. I was social, outgoing, the life of the party. My insecurities diminished. And every empty bottle made the inner wolf stronger.

Soon, my drinking turned into partying. I frequented nightclubs and similar scenes. My work ethic was still in place. I was still supporting my family. But my heart was becoming callous.

Lori and I began to drift apart, as I faded further and further into the darkness of the nightlife. Sure, I still brought home the money. But it was as if I was sending it in my place. Money was my cold and impersonal liaison.

The party lifestyle swiftly swallowed me whole. I was a prisoner of pleasure. An emotional chasm laid between Lori and I. Its depths were too menacing to brave. So my marriage was misplaced, yielding its rightful position to the mistress of the nightlife. Immersed in the riotous scene, I began to do things of which I am now ashamed.

The wolf was alive and on the prowl.

The pace of it all wasted me away. There was no satisfaction. Like a castaway, lost at sea, I was desperately trying to quench my thirst for pleasure, drinking salty ocean water that only caused a greater thirst within me. My problem, though I didn't exactly see it as one at the time, only grew worse.

Even though I would always come home, Lori knew what was happening.

The culmination of it all, the indication of just how bad things had become, happened one miserable night. While seeking the affection of my wife, I was rejected. Knowing the filth with which I had been flirting, Lori turned a despondent shoulder to me. Angered and insulted, drunk and foolish, I physically retaliated against her rejection. I hit her. I hit my wife.

The wolf bit, and the wolf bit hard.

All that I had seen and hated as a child, I had now become. The curse had come full circle. The dark harvest yielded its bitter fruit. But even that was not enough to break the spell that the party lifestyle had veiled over my undiscerning eyes.

My problem continued to grow worse. But I was tough. I was in charge. I was still working hard. So, in my mind, I was a man. But even that man had his fears.

One night, after the usual debauchery, I didn't go home at all. In a haze, I woke up in some apartment somewhere. Panicked thoughts rushed through my mind, ringing like loud and blaring alarms: "Where am I? What did I do? Lori is going to kill me!" Fear rushed me to my feet. I had to get home right away.

Little did I know, Lori had been up all night, worrying about me. She recalls, "I was calling hospitals, wondering if something happened to him. I thought, 'something better have happened to him.'"

It was at this point that I was sure Lori would leave me. When I got home, arguing ensued. I don't exactly recall all of the unfortunate details of that argument, but I felt that my marriage was soon coming to an end. Something told me that Lori would leave me.

But, in the middle of our passionate exchange, our phone rang. It was from my mom's house. On the other end of that line was unexpected and tragic news. It was about one of my brothers. He died.

My brother was heavily affected by long-term drug use. His mind was wiped, his eyes were heavy and his movement was lethargic. At the time, he lived at a mental institution as an outpatient sharing a room with another patient. There was a mix up with his medication. Either they gave him the wrong kind of medication or the wrong dosage of medication. Whatever the mix-up, my brother fell asleep and never woke up again.

Lori and I stopped arguing and we drove to my mom's house.

I was still so caught up in myself that I couldn't even mourn the death of my brother. That's how lost I was. In fact, I was laughing on the inside, quite pleased that I had evaded Lori's anger and gained her sympathy instead. I said to myself, "I can't believe I got away with that! What timing!" If I had a conscience, it was dead.

When we arrived at my mother's house, my family greeted us. And when I was asked about where I was the night before, I smugly responded, "Oh, you know how it is." The men of the family jovially agreed.

That incident didn't change me, and Lori stayed.

Fast forward to 1980. My first son, Paulie, was born. And yet my partying continued, and my marriage problems grew much worse.

It wasn't until another death of a loved one that I began to experience things that actually began to melt away the ice that froze my conscience. Actually, it was the spiritual death of my brother. He died to himself and became alive to Christ.

My brother, Alfred, and my sister-in-law had become Christians. Now, to appreciate such a miracle, you must know that Alfred was just like me. And, according to my wife, Alfred was actually worse than me. Can you believe that? That's intense!

But the old Alfred had died. And there was a new, peculiar man in the place of the brother I knew. And he preached to me! I didn't want to hear it. I believe Alfred was given a double portion anointing – he needed it to preach to me. But you know how it goes when someone gets saved. They want their whole family to experience the freedom and newness of life. So, Alfred had the church begin to pray for me.

Something strange began to happen. It was something that had not happened in a very long time. Before, when I would party, I was lost in the ecstasy of the thrill. But now, I was hindered. I felt a slight prick in my conscience. The convicting power of the Holy Spirit began to overshadow everything I did. Before long, I didn't just feel a slight discomfort of the soul. I began to feel the overwhelmingly nasty and vile effects of my sin. I just felt plain nasty.

But I continued in it anyway.

Every Sunday, my brother would call my home to invite my family and I to church. He called so often that it got to the point where Lori and I would argue about who would answer the phone to reject the invitation. Alfred was very persistent, a hound dog of Heaven.

But Alfred eventually said something that grabbed my attention. One day, he looked at me and frankly said, "You know, Paul, God can save your marriage." That certainly struck my interest.

After being invited several times, Lori and I finally went to church. And something unlikely happened - we began to follow Alfred from church to church. Soon, Lori and I each committed to Christ but on different occasions.

Lori got saved after a night at Shakey's Pizza. She can pinpoint the time and date. Alfred had told her, "If the rapture happens while you sleep, you'll wake up in the morning and the kids will be gone." Needless to say, she didn't want to be left behind without the kids. That notion put the fear of God in her. And she got saved.

But, as for me, I don't really know the exact moment of my transformation. Back then, I pretty much "got saved" every time I went to church. There are actually a few dozen preachers who claim me as their convert. The problem was that even though, at church, I would commit myself to Heaven, after leaving church, I would just go live like Hell again.

If ever I could successfully or accurately identify a single moment that marked my true conversion, a turning point, it would be one Friday night in particular.

One night, while waiting at home for my brother to pick me up to go clubbing, I was met by an unexpected moment of clarity. I was dressed up and already pre-gaming with a few drinks and some disco music. My intended plans for the evening were not exactly reflective of my developing Christianity. But, still, God speaks to sinners.

Prepared for a night of my usual revelry, I stood waiting in my home's hallway. The disruptive disco music seemed to fade into my unawareness, as I caught a glimpse of my faithful and patient wife. She looked beautiful, almost saintly. My glimpse at her stirred in me an uneasy and overwhelming sense of guilt. In that moment, I sobered up in more ways than one. Staring at Lori, I asked myself a question that was long overdue: "What am I doing?"

God had been working on my heart for a while.

But, in that moment, I prayed a child-like and almost silly prayer. Remembering all that Alfred had told me about God, I said, "God, my brother says that you're good and that you can help me. If you can, I'll give you a chance."

It was a simple prayer, but that was all I needed. The two years that came after that moment were life altering.

#2 The Law of Covenant

Though I wasn't an expert at being spiritual, God heard my simple prayer. That's because God is into making deals.

I consider the Holy Spirit to be my business partner, and my relationship with God has been peppered with pacts between He and I. Now, of course, I do not wish to give you the impression that God is some sort of a celestial genie. However, He does respond to genuine prayers of faith. And we are instructed to not be foolish in making vows to God.

"When you make a promise to God, don't delay in following through, for God takes no pleasure in fools. Keep all the promises you make to him."

~ Ecclesiastes 5:4

If you're going to make a deal with God, you had better keep up your end. Don't be apathetic in your approach toward Him. Let your prayers be filled with a holy and trembling reverence. And let not a single one of the words that you speak to Him be spoken in haste. But also know that making a covenant with God can lead to prosperity.

God did end up saving my marriage, and I did keep good on my promise to serve Him. I do not regret making my simple, faith-filled covenant with God.

Jesus even references the wideness of God's generosity.

"Yes, ask me for anything in my name, and I will do it!"

~ John 14:14

So don't be filled with fear. Be filled with faith. Approach God. If He prospers your business, will you promise to fund the Kingdom? If He helps you get out of debt, with you be more wise with your finances? If He increases you, will you support the gospel with your increase? Tell Him so, and see what He does.

The Law of Covenant: God can be approached with deals.

Chapter 2
Divine Destiny

We were looking for a church. But each church that Lori and I visited just didn't seem to be the right fit. We were never really able to build strong relationships in any of the churches that we frequented, and there was a certain sense of discomfort that we felt when attending those churches. I don't mean that there was anything wrong with the churches per se. Rather, we just didn't feel like we were supposed to be there. And, truly, God was pulling us elsewhere.

I remember one very discouraging occurrence in particular. At that time, though I was experiencing some transformation in my life, I was still in need of a spiritual breakthrough. Yet I was convicted and longing for greater transformation. I *really* wanted to change. But, having grown up in the kind of home I grew up in, I wasn't very good at showing my emotions, sharing my feelings or opening up about my issues. You might remember, for example, that I was taught that men don't cry.

The inability to truly connect on this level kept me from forming healthy church relationships. I was calling out for help but didn't know how to be heard.

Lori and I had become somewhat settled at a certain church. We were the only Hispanic family in the church and, to be honest, I strongly suspected that some key members in that church were prejudice. Other than for church sporting events, we were not engaged or contacted. But I had to try to connect.

Eventually, after much inner wrestling, I worked up the courage to approach someone for help and friendship. I was ready to be open, humble and honest about my issues. With a hesitant and quiet demeanor, I approached a certain man who I had come to see as somewhat of a role model. I was in a trial and I wanted freedom from sin. So, for the first time in my life, I opened up. Contrary to what I had been taught as a child, I timidly reached for a helping hand. I made myself vulnerable. But after I had finished sharing what was on my heart, the man responded with a condescending sneer and told me, "I've got my problems. You have yours." His words shook me. By his response, I was heavily discouraged. Speechless and with my head hung low, I walked away from that short conversation.

Though we had attended that church for three months, we never once met the pastor. We were faithful too. We would go outreaching in the ghettos and bring several visitors to the church. But, in such instances, we were told, "We don't want *those* kind of people here."

Lori and I eventually sensed that it was time for us to leave that church. Burned and offended, we decided that we would no longer attend church. We told ourselves, "We'll just watch Christian television."

It was some time later that my family had invited us to join them on a vacation in Baja, CA – Rosarito. We were actually planning on going, but Lori, at the same time, had discovered that her car's tags were expired. And it was a new car, so the tags were not cheap. Lori and I are sticklers when it comes to paying the bills. So, because of the unexpected financial obligation, we were left without any extra money, and we were forced to decline the invitation for vacation.

But when we declined the invitation, my family insisted on us going. What was unusual was that they offered to pay! They never paid for anything like that. Neither had they ever made such a generous offer. I took note of the abnormal situation.

Why had they offered to pay? Though a loving family, it was so unlike them. Still, Lori and I refused to go on that trip. My family pressed further by trying to guilt me into going for "the sake of mom and dad."

But we stood firmly on our decision to not go on this particular trip. My family vacationed without us.

Still, I was puzzled by my family's insistence. That nagging sense of bewilderment lingered.

During the time that my family was away on that vacation, Lori and I decided to attend a family BBQ, a gathering for the father of one of our friends. You know, it was something to do.

The BBQ took place at a house in the high desert. As Lori and I were driving up to the house, we saw two men standing out in the front yard. I immediately recognized them. Before I had started going to church, I used to drink their wine and smoke their dope. They were partiers just like me.

Even now, they had an air of inebriation about them. They were loose, relaxed and emitted a glow of gladness. I told Lori, "These guys are high to the max! They're stoned! Just look at them!" Lori laughed.

Once parked and situated, Lori and I mingled with friends. I eventually approached the two men who were giving off such elevated vibes.

Now, I've never been one to mince words. If you want honesty, hang around me. I call it like I see it, and I don't deal out flattery. So when I greeted the two men, my undiminished words shot out from my mouth like bullets – it was friendly fire: "You guys look high to the max!"

Their response surprised me. "Oh, we're high alright, but it's not what you think." I thought to myself, "a new drug perhaps." They clarified, "We're high on Jesus!"

Keep in mind that I had just come out of my church search and, at that point, found church to be unappealing. My former experience had turned me off to the whole idea. As far as I had decided, I was a Christian all on my own. I wanted nothing to do with a church or church people.

But, as my conversation with these two men progressed, I found myself attracted to their "Aura", as some would say. And the more they talked, the more curious I became. There was just something different about them. What they carried was unique to anything that I had ever known. They weren't like the other Christians with whom I had come into contact. On them was stamped a strong mark of authenticity. And these weren't the men

I had once known. They seemed to have undergone extreme transformation.

In fact, when I used to party with them, they would leave early to ensure that they made it to Bible study. But that hypocrisy was now gone. They explained to me that they had been "set free" from all of that. These were truly different men; they had changed.

My curiosity reached its peak. I knew that I wanted what they had. So I inquired, "What happened to you guys?"

They began to tell me about their encounters with the Holy Spirit and how God had set them free. Naturally, that led them to invite me to church.

"We go to a church called Praise Chapel", they informed me.

Later the next week, impressed by the transformation that I saw in the two men, I went searching for their church. I went to scope out the church on a weekday afternoon when there was no church service in progress. I told myself that I was only going to take a look at it.

The church was located in an area with which I was very familiar, but I was unable to find it. I checked the address, looked around and then double-checked the address. After experiencing a great deal of difficulty trying to find the church, I started to wonder if there really was a church in that area.

I picked up a phone and called my wife: "There's no church here, Lori!" But before I could finish the phone call, I caught a glimpse of a seemingly misplaced sign. The sign read,

Pentecostal Church
Pastor Johnny Dorris
Sundays at 10:00am
Wednesdays at 7:00pm

And then I realized, "Oh my goodness – it's a house!" It was actually a regular house that was converted into a church. I had never seen a church like it before. I was used to seeing actual church buildings, furnished with fancy and grandeur. There was no steeple and no stained glass windows. It was just a house with an orange sign. This was definitely different. I took a look and then drove away.

A couple more weeks passed. Then Lori and I decided to finally visit that odd little church, that little house with an orange sign.

The memory of my visit is still vivid. The day was a hot one – 110 degrees to be exact. And in that scorching weather, I wore my Sunday best - a suit and tie. Hot, uncomfortable, agitated and impatient, Lori and I showed up late. So all of the good seats were taken. People packed the inside of the building and began overflowing onto the porch. And that porch was so packed that it looked like it would collapse.

Anticipating discomfort, Lori made it very clear to me: "I'm not sitting outside. If we have to sit outside, I'm leaving." I agreed. We reluctantly got out of the car and began a mellow pace toward the church. To our surprise, someone met us on the steps of the porch and informed us that there were seats for us inside. Puzzled, Lori and I were delighted. Apparently, someone saw us pull up and noticed that we were visitors.

I don't remember much about the preaching or the details of that church service, but I remember this: right after the worship portion of the service, the pastor welcomed everyone. He then stepped off of the platform, walked right up to us and said, "Hello. I'm Johnny Dorris. Welcome to Praise Chapel." This was a major difference. At the other churches that we attended (some for weeks), we never met the pastors. But at that little church, the senior pastor welcomed us within only minutes of us being there. It blew my mind.

Then Johnny Dorris, while standing back on the platform, spoke these powerful words to the congregation – these words I will never forget: "If you're good enough for God, you're good enough for us." When he spoke those words, I immediately thought of the church that told us to stop bringing people from those ghetto apartment complexes. What a contrast. This was truly a loving church.

And I was locked in.

It wasn't the preaching, the worship, the style of the building or the charisma of the pastor that gripped my heart. It was a seat, a handshake and simple, welcoming words.

It could have been otherwise. Imagine if they had not given up the seats for us. How many churches lose people because of these little issues? It's amazing how someone's entire life destiny can be tied to someone else's simple act of consideration – giving up a chair, speaking a kind word, a handshake. Even the way we greet people is important. Where would my life be today had we left the church that day? I don't know who gave up their seats for me, but their gesture may very well have indirectly saved my soul.

Destiny can seem so fragile, but, when you're guided by the merciful hand of God, you can't miss it. In hindsight, I see clearly. Little things make a big difference. Now I know why my family insisted on Lori and I going on vacation with them.

It was all spiritual warfare. God mapped a path for us, and the enemy was trying to detour us from it. Had we gone on vacation, we would not have met up with those two men. Had we not met up with those two men, we would have never found Praise Chapel, the church that became our home for true discipleship.

Chapter 3
Taming the Wolf

L ori and I were now locked into an amazing church, living under the guidance of a loving pastor and genuinely pursuing the will of God. The journey of discipleship had begun. It was during this time that I learned my first lesson in giving. My generous lifestyle started very basic. It began with tithing.

But when I first began to truly commit to God and church, my giving toward God was more of a tip than an investment. Sure, I gave, but my giving was neither consistent nor generous. If I were to be feeling especially big-hearted, I might throw in a crispy $5 bill. I was skeptical, closed to the idea of giving to the church and rather protective of my own. As far as I was concerned, nobody was going to pull a quick one on me, especially not some greasy, manipulative preacher. Though happy with my pastor, I had my secret, subtle suspicions that he was possibly a charlatan. Yes, I was really defensive.

But, at that point, could you really blame me?

At the time, because I was a hard worker, I was making anywhere from $4,000 to $6,000 a month. So I was almost appalled at the idea of not only sowing tithes but also giving an offering on top of that. The calculations alone made me angry. I thought, "That's $400 to $500 a check! And I get paid bi-weekly."

But God was working on my heart, and paying my tithes would be my first test in the area of faith and finance.

At first, money flowed from my wallet like L.A. traffic through a busy morning. However, I was slowly beginning to catch on. Feeling as if I were scrooge on Christmas morning, I noticed that my heart began to change. But this was no instant transformation. My grip on my cash loosened gradually. I knew I was in the wrong, and the principle of the tithe intrigued me.

"'Bring all the tithes into the storehouse so there will be enough food in my Temple. If you do,' says the LORD of Heaven's Armies, 'I will open the windows of heaven for you. I will pour out a blessing so great you won't have enough room to take it in! Try it! Put me to the test!'"

~ Malachi 3:10

Now I understand that some believers might consider the tithe to be an Old Testament concept that should be now discontinued. But Jesus Himself lends us His thoughts on the matter.

"You should tithe, yes, but do not neglect the more important things."

~ Matthew 23:23b

Whether or not others want to believe in tithing, I am certain of two things: Firstly, tithing is all about recognizing God's sovereign ownership over all one possesses. And, secondly, I'd be very glad to take someone's blessing if they don't want it. I'll tithe, and God will give to me what should have been theirs. Was that not what happened in the case of the unfaithful servant?

"Then he ordered, 'Take the money from this servant, and give it to the one with the ten bags of silver."

~ Matthew 25:28

Also, personal experience powerfully pleads of the tithe's enduring legitimacy. The bottom line is this: tithing works just as the scripture said it would. That leads me to conclude that the blessing of the tithe is still Biblical.

And I found that to be true.

At the start of my tithing lifestyle, I tithed through my wife. I didn't even want to see the checks. Each time that I saw the amounts that I was giving to the church, I cringed, imagining what might have been. I would think, "That could have been used for a vacation." Lori would write the check and drop it in the basket. And if she didn't do it quickly, there was a very good chance that I would have changed my calculating mind.

But God began to give back. Very rapidly, my finances increased. God was faithful to meet His promise to open the windows of Heaven, windows that have been wide open ever since.

#3 The Law of Firsts

My lesson in tithing was important, because it gave me the proper perspective: everything I have is God's. God owns it all. To that notion, some defensively reply, "Well, I worked for what I have!" And that's true. But who gave them the ability to work? Who gave them a mind to focus on their work? Who gave them the hands to carry out their work? You gave them existence without which they couldn't be at work?

42

Once you accept that everything belongs to Him, you gain the right perspective. You won't feel robbed giving to God when you realize that He is letting you keep most of what's His for yourself. The scripture instructs us to give of our firsts, not of our leftovers.

"Upon the first *day* of the week let every one of you lay by him in store, as *God* hath prospered him, that there be no gatherings when I come."

~ 1 Corinthians 16:2

From the scripture above, I want you to extract two truths. Firstly, God is the one who prospers us. Secondly, Paul the apostle instructed the Corinthians to give on the first day of the week. Before they were to carry on with the rest of the week's spending, they were to first invest in the Kingdom of God.

Okay, now I really want to challenge you. We say, "God, I'll give when you bless me." But God says, "I'll bless you when you give." We wait until we get a promotion to give. But God waits until we give to promote us. How many times have you withheld from the Kingdom to see if you could first take care of yourself? I know this seems harsh, but the road to prosperity is not an easy one. God will always test you before He will bless you.

Do you wait until the end of the month to give to God? Do you give to Him from the top or scrape up for Him from the bottom? Does He get your first or your worst?

I like the way that Jesus put it. In fact, this is my favorite Bible verse. I have it written over the entryway of my church's sanctuary:

"But seek ye first the kingdom of God, and his righteousness; and all these things shall be added unto you."

~ Matthew 6:33

God is not going to abandon you. If you will focus on the Kingdom, God will focus on your needs. He doesn't ask this of us just to be cruel. God wants to teach you how to manage what He has given to you, so that He can begin to entrust you with more. It comes down to a simple choice: faith or fear. Fear gives God the leftovers. Faith gives God the best.

The Law of Firsts: God prospers those who give their first and best to Him.

So I continued to attend church on a regular basis. I was taught the importance of fellowship and connecting with other believers. I was learning to open up and allow others to truly know me.

I began to tithe. As you know, at first, I resisted the idea. But I soon learned that my money wasn't really my money. It was always God's money.

My marriage was improving as I developed into a model Christian. Things were stabilizing and my life was beginning to truly change. The flame of hope was rekindled in my heart, though maybe just an ember for the time.

I was committed enough to be appreciated but not yet committed enough to be inconvenienced. I was enjoying my new Christian lifestyle. But God was about to send tremors and shockwaves throughout the comfortable grounds of my convenient Christian life. He was calling me to deeper realms of commitment.

Pastor Johnny Dorris approached me one day and began to talk to me about something called a "church planting conference". I wondered what on earth it was all about.

You see, the church I attended was a part of what is known as a "church multiplication movement", a worldwide network of churches that evangelize, disciple within and send people to start new churches ("pioneer churches"). Ideally, every church eventually grows to begin planting more churches. Thus, there is multiplication. Someone who decides to respond to the call, start a church and become a pastor is said to be "sent out".

And, amazingly, at every conference, people were sent out. In such a movement, it is very difficult to remain unchallenged concerning the call of God. In fact, the mission statement of the fellowship was, "Win. Build. Send."

So my pastor invited me to the Praise Chapel world conference. At that conference, new pioneer churches were announced and christened. And all of the conference speakers spoke in a constant theme: the call of God, radical obedience, sacrifice, church-planting and such.

Advised by my pastor and sponsored by the church, I felt somewhat of an obligation to go to the conference. But I really didn't want to go. For starters, I still very much felt like an outsider. I didn't understand any of the terminology that people used when discussing the conference. It was uncomfortably unfamiliar. And the conference was to last an entire week. To me, that was really long for a conference.

Plus, I was scared. I wondered if I was supposed to go and pastor a church that week. Questions ran through my troubled mind: "Am I going to get 'sent out'? Do they want me to give my life? My house?"

I had just finally come to find a church that I actually liked! And they were already talking about me leaving. It seemed as though the honeymoon was over. The reality of Christianity was beginning to unfold before me. I discovered that it was a call to sacrifice, a commitment for which I must pay a high price.

#4 The Law of Knowledge

What I didn't know about Christianity was holding me back. I thought that if I went to that conference, I would be forced to become miserable. In other words, I let my ignorance inspire fear.

What you don't know can be binding you. The things you don't understand can be limiting you. The things about which you are unaware can sneak up on you. Knowledge leads to prosperity. In fact, knowledge is so powerful that it can bring about ultimate freedom.

"And you will know the truth, and the truth will set you free."

~ **John 8:32**

The truth will set you free. I wonder how many believers are only a fact away from freedom. I wonder how many are missing prosperity by only an ounce of ignorance. I wonder how much of your frustration comes from simply not knowing what to do.

Knowledge brings breakthrough. Knowledge brings freedom. Knowledge removes boundaries. Indeed, the old cliché is false, for, as a matter of fact, what you don't know does hurt you. Information eliminates ignorance.

Do you study the Word of God? Do you learn from people you consider successful? Do you expand your mind through reading and exploration? How much of what God has for you goes unclaimed simply because you don't know about it?

Learners grow. The day you stop learning is the day you become stuck. Knowledge, especially of God's Word, will shatter the walls of frustration, and remove the stubborn barriers of entrapment.

The Law of Knowledge: The more you know the further you go.

Of course, Lori talked me into going. So we went.

The day sessions were held at a little church in Maywood, CA. The night sessions were held at a high school auditorium. And the messages were getting to me. I had never been so discomforted in my life! God was doing something very deep within me. I began to see, for the first time ever, the depths of self-denial. And God started messing with my pride.

I loved my security. And I loved the security that I provided for my family. It's what I had known since I was a kid: a man provides security. God was indeed challenging me!

During the conference, Lori and I went to lunch with a few friends and my pastor. While we were enjoying our meals, our conversation found its way to the topic of work. Seated at the table with us was one of my co-workers. My co-worker, who was also a part of Praise Chapel and was attending the conference, asked me a very simple question: "Paul, what's the most secure position in the company?" Of course, I knew the answer. Now, I don't remember what I told him, but I do remember what my pastor told me. After I gave a satisfactory answer to my co-worker, Pastor Johnny began to playfully mock me. He teased, "Oh, here's Mr. Security!" The comment was funny, but it pricked my ego.

I was provoked to anger and frustration. I huffed internally, "I'm a man, and pastor Johnny disrespected me!" And, to be honest, had it been anyone else to make such a remark at my expense, I would have knocked him out.

Pastor Johnny's taunts continued all throughout the week. In hindsight, I can see what he was doing. But, at the time, I was mad, and I was mad for several reasons. I was mad because Lori convinced me to go to that conference. I was mad because it was too long. I was mad because my pastor was provoking me. All week long with that! "Mr. Security this" and "Mr. Security that." The messages were getting to me – they challenged me. Internal tension was building.

The speakers kept calling me to greater sacrifice. My pastor teased my pride in my own security. I felt that I was either going to kill someone or blow up! I was just waiting for the conference to end.

And… I was ready to beat up Johnny Dorris.

Back in my hotel room, I paced with anger, as my wife tried to calm me. It all seemed like too much. Something was going to happen.

But I didn't beat up Johnny Dorris, though I *really* wanted to.

I didn't kill anyone. I really *didn't* want to.

I didn't go home. It wasn't practical.

And I didn't lash out in anger, as I had done in times past.

Instead, I leaned on my wife

… and wept.

This man, who had been taught to never cry, who had set a wall against everyone, wept.

God. Broke. Me.

I cried until about 2 in the morning. And I didn't just cry. I sobbed. My selfish pride, my big ego, my burning anger – they all crumbled. They all dissolved, as I stood there in a state a vulnerability that I had never before known. True and deep transformation was finally taking place. All that I was – a partier, a drunk, a man's man – was changed.

The wolf was dead.

With every tear that fell down my face, I was being molded. And I sensed the gentle breeze of God's Holy Spirit. What a miracle, that I could be changed. I felt a joy, a peace and a certainty. What did that to me? It wasn't security. It was a blessed assurance. That wasn't the strength of man. It was the fortitude of God.

The change that was occurring within me was nothing short of miraculous. If you only knew what kind of man I was! That God would still love me, that He would even take the time to transform my heart – that is love beyond compare.

As I laid my head down on my pillow that night, I was a new man. That night, God gave me visions. I saw myself preaching before crowds of people. I saw myself traveling the nations of the world. I saw my family alongside me in church and in ministry. The visions were so real that I thought I had perhaps been translated into the future.

And when I woke up, I was fired up! I had been endowed with a Heavenly newness. I was baptized in the Holy Spirit. I had never before felt such liberty. The weight of my past burdens was lifted. There was an energy, a freshness about the morning. It was my brand new start.

When I returned from the conference, I was truly a different man. I didn't want to kill Johnny Dorris anymore. In fact, I now see that he was the match that lit a fire in me.

I sat down with him and told him that I was ready for all of that "discipleship stuff". I said, "Disciple me. Confront me. Be involved in my life. Get in my face if you have to. I'm ready to do this. I give you permission to pastor me."

#5 The Law of Honor and Humility

Honoring my pastor opened up a world of blessing for me. Ego will often keep people from giving proper honor to those who deserve it. And, no, we are not to submit to the dictatorship of controlling men. Rather, I am writing of the honor that the scripture tells us to give.

"Render therefore to all their dues: tribute to whom tribute *is due*; custom to whom custom; fear to whom fear; honour to whom honour."

~ Romans 13:7

Honor and humility are always found together. I cannot honor anyone if I am not humble enough to admit that honor is due to them. But when you, in humility, give honor where it's do, a world of opportunities will present itself to you.

It's quite possible that your dishonor of someone is keeping you from prosperity. Do you honor your employer? Do you honor your teacher? Do you honor your pastor? Sure, some people in positions of authority act in ways that inspire disdain. But, when you demonstrate honor, you are ultimately honoring God.

Honor is the knob on the door of opportunity. Lying to, stealing from (even time theft), gossiping about and disrespectfully conflicting with people of authority is dishonorable. When you dishonor someone, you cut yourself off from the blessings that God wants to give you through them. Not only can dishonor sever your potentially beneficially relationships, but it can also reflect poorly upon you, bringing a bad testimony to Christianity. And your dishonor toward someone else may inspire dishonor toward you in those who are under your authority.

The Law of Honor and Humility: Humility demonstrated through honor opens doors that lead to your destiny.

When I began to truly honor the guidance and leadership of my pastor, I developed as a committed follower of Christ.

And my commitment surprised even me. Lori and I focused on the call of God. We no longer held anything back. In total self-abandonment, we pursued to live in radical obedience toward Christ. Like a nightmare that fades into forgetfulness as you awake, so my past was becoming a fuzzy, distant reality. I was truly awake, and the nightmare was losing its grip on me.

Even still, there were challenges to be faced and tests to be passed. As I had written earlier, I was, at one point, hesitant to support the church financially. I suppose it was because of suspicion and distrust. And, of course, it was also partly because I worked so hard for my money.

Dear reader, I want you to know that God will test you the hardest in the areas that He wants to bless you the most. And, unknown to me at the time, God had called me to become a steward of Kingdom finances. So Lori and I faced what I have come to refer to as, "money tests". Each test is really a test in faith. But there are many aspects to faith – trust, persistence, faithfulness and so on.

One of the first tests that I had to take came at a time when I really didn't have much to give. God typically tests us in ways that require the most faith. His tests stretch our faith.

I was tithing and then some. Working for a telephone company, I was an employee, not a company owner. So the money I made was based on the time that I invested into the company.

The telephone company I worked for had its own retail program. We could buy things from the company based on credit. This included television sets, radios and various other things. I often used the credit system to afford new electronics.

One Sunday, Pastor Johnny Dorris announced that we would be taking pledges for the church. He explained that each member was encouraged to commit to giving a certain amount over a certain period of time. Some pledged $500 over six months. Others pledged $100 over three months. People pledged according to both their own faith and ability.

While considering what Lori and I would pledge, God spoke a very clear number to my heart. He often does this with me. In fact, He often does this with many believers. But most ignore such prompting and instead settle for what they deem to be reasonable. In doing so, they fail the test and must repeat the course again.

And it is to their detriment that many disobey the voice of the Holy Spirit. For God always challenges us to grow us and promote us. If we cannot obey His minor instructions, we will never grow to the place where we can receive His major ones.

Lori and I determined, early on, that we would never say "no" to God. But what God spoke to me at the time was, in my opinion, impossible. But His instructions were clear. As Pastor Johnny was carrying on with the church pledge presentation, God spoke to me a number.

...$1,000

"A thousand dollars? I don't have one thousand dollars", I told the Lord. Was I mishearing God? Was it perhaps the Devil trying to get me to be foolish with my finances? Could it have been an emotional response? My mind looked for an excuse to which it could successfully cling. I wanted to be sure that it was truly God.

For, in fact, I did not have a thousand dollars. What was I to do? And then the Lord challenged me further. His Words cut deep: "You borrow money to buy television sets. Borrow $1,000." Many would dismiss that direction. But I knew it was God. So I did just that. I borrowed $1,000 from a credit union to pledge to the church. And you know what?

... I'm still alive.

My family didn't starve. My bills were all paid. The old me would have never submitted to God. And the old me would have never obtained Heaven's prosperity. That was one test passed with many more to come.

#6 The Law of Faith

This place in my story might be as good a place as any to insert this law, the law of faith. Really, this law is so fundamental to prosperity that it could have been inserted at any place in this book. All the laws of prosperity, at their base, are mounted upon this essential. Faith is inseparable from every element of prosperity.

Faith is trust in action, belief at work and conviction in motion. Without faith, you can't please, receive from or even become aware of God. If prosperity is a house then faith is the foundation.

Faith is the door between the earthly and Heavenly realm. It is what connects you with God's resources. By faith, we step outside of human limitation and into God's infinite ability.

Much of what seems to hold you back, what seems to cause calamity and disorder, simply stems from a lack of faith. Of course, the life of faith is not without its troubles, for Jesus Himself said the believer would face diverse trials. But the life of faith is one of purpose and power.

While the topic of faith is itself both deserving of and able to fill another book entirely, I do want to focus your attention on one Biblical figure who uniquely exemplifies faith: Abraham.

"For the Scriptures tell us, 'Abraham believed God, and God counted him as righteous because of his faith.'"
~ Romans 4:3

In Judaism, Abraham is considered to be a patriarch, the founding father of Israel's covenant with God. It was through Abraham that God made a special and enduring covenant with the Jewish people. Circumcision marked said covenant.

Paul the apostle also notes Abraham as being a model or example, a forerunner who was among the first to share with God a special relationship based on faith. His relationship with God served as somewhat of a prototype for all future believers. According to the scripture, this new covenant is not marked by circumcision but by faith.

Because of his faith, Abraham is the father of the nation of Israel and one of the first to experience righteousness by faith. Abraham's story is truly amazing.

Abraham was seventy-five years old when he received a challenging command from God. He was told to leave his home and go to a land that God would show him. God promised Abraham that his obedience would position him to father an entire nation of offspring. Abraham didn't delay. He moved. Without knowing his destination, Abraham began his journey.

But this wasn't the kind of move that could be done with a couple trips in a U-Haul truck. Abraham was a very wealthy and well-established man. The Bible notes,

"(Abram was very rich in livestock, silver, and gold.)"
~ Genesis 13:2

Abraham left the comforts of his established dominion to follow the voice of God. Abraham didn't have a plan except to obey God.

Abraham, his wife, his family, his servants, his livestock and his possessions moved around for quite some time. God told Abraham that he and his wife, Sarah, would have a son, a son through whom

Abraham would become the father of many nations. Because of their old age, Abraham and Sarah thought it unbelievable that they would have a child. But Abraham believed God, and God kept good on His promise. With Sarah, Abraham eventually had his son, Isaac.

Fast-forward a bit. The Lord decided to test the heart of Abraham, demanding that Isaac be sacrificed. Abraham, obedient to the voice of God, prepared Isaac to be sacrificed. But, while Abraham obliged, God mercifully stopped the sacrifice and saw that Abraham was willing to obey. Abraham passed an important test. God wanted to see if Abraham would prioritize the Giver over the blessing.

I want to point out three different ways that Abraham demonstrated his faith in God:

1. Abraham had the faith to risk.
2. Abraham had the faith to trust.
3. Abraham had the faith to surrender.

Firstly, Abraham had faith to risk (**Genesis 12:1-20**). What did he risk? He risked everything. Remember, Abraham was wealthy even before God had called him. Yet, when God spoke to him, Abraham didn't hesitate or waver. He immediately packed his things and moved.

Do you have the faith to risk? Don't expect the blessing of Abraham without demonstrating the faith of Abraham. Don't expect God to give you reward without risk. Without even knowing specifically where God was taking him, Abraham put everything that he had on the line to follow after God's call on his life.

Secondly, Abraham had the faith to trust God (**Genesis 17:1-27**). Though he and his wife were in their later years of life, though it seemed near impossible for him to father another child, Abraham trusted God. He didn't let his circumstance limit his faith in God's ability.

In what do you place more of your faith: God's Word or your current predicament? What brings challenge to men can't inspire even a second thought in God. While people are running around and losing their calm, God sits on His throne and develops a robust plan. It's time to move out of fear and into faith. Relax. Be at peace. Trust God. He knows what He's doing.

Finally, Abraham had the faith to surrender (**Genesis 22:1-19**). Though Isaac was a gift from God, he was called upon as a sacrifice. Abraham could have argued with God, pleading, "Lord, why would you take away what you promised to me? Why would you bless me just to remove it from me? It makes no sense!"

But, often, God will bless you just to test you. He wants to see how tightly we grip His gifts. Do you put what God has provided and promised as priority over what He asks? Do your blessings obstruct obedience? Abraham knew that, even without Isaac (who seemed to be the only realistic key to the fulfillment of the promise), God was able to make a way. When your understanding cannot grasp God's commands and decrees, it's time to surrender.

I admire Abraham, and I aspire to that grand kind of faith. I hope that you too note Abraham as a worthy role model.

The Law of Faith: Faith reveals, step by step, the progressive path to prosperity.

And, certainly, I needed faith of my own. For after four years of faithful service to our church and by the awesome grace of God, Lori and I became assistant pastors. Yes, I know. That's a miracle. God is amazing! But you know what they say?

New levels, new devils.

Chapter 4
An Unfamiliar Land

Mission trips, Bible studies and church ministry – Lori and I were faithful to our new position as assistant pastors. But two years later, we were to take yet another step of radical faith. Recall that church planting conference I attended. Well, we continued to attend that conference every year. And, once having disdained the conference, in August of 1989, Lori and I attended it yet again. Only that time, we were announced as pioneer pastors. That is to say that Lori and I were being "sent out". We were taking over a little church in Hayward, CA.

Hayward is roughly a 6 hour drive from Ontario – 400 miles away. I liken my experience to the one Abraham had. We had to leave our church, our family, our friends and our old life. I quit my job, rented out my house and said a farewell to my parents and siblings – they all lived in Southern California. As I drove up the 5 freeway, I knew that I had no job waiting for me in Hayward. All the money I possessed was in my back pocket. I had not even a single connection in the new land. Upon recollection, I can't help but thinking of the verse:

"And everyone who has given up houses or brothers or sisters or father or mother or children or property, for my sake, will receive a hundred times as much in return and will inherit eternal life."

~ Matthew 19:29

Lori and I were living it. But I'm going to be honest with you. It was difficult to do. Some said that we were crazy. After all, who drags their family 400 miles away to leave security? That's a crazy move for "Mr. Security", isn't it? We were heartbroken to leave, but the call of God was before us. We, of course, took the kids with us. Even my dog Chavela came along for the adventure. She was a mutt and a half, but she was a pioneer too.

To help the emotional transition, we intentionally had no communication with our home church for six months.

#7 The Law of Obedience

Asking for God's blessing while you walk in disobedience is like trying to keep your boat afloat while drilling holes in it. Let's look again at the life of Abraham. This is what the Bible says about obedience:

> **"Now the LORD said to Abram,**
> **'Go forth from your country,**
> **And from your relatives**
> **And from your father's house,**
> **To the land which I will show you;**
> **And I will make you a great nation,**
> **And I will bless you,**
> **And make your name great;**
> **And so you shall be a blessing;**
> **And I will bless those who bless you,**
> **And the one who curses you I will curse.**
> **And in you all the families of the earth will be blessed.'"**
> **~ Genesis 12:1-3**

Now we already looked at the faith behind Abraham's obedience, and, remember, faith is foundational to all of the laws of prosperity. But obedience is the animation of faith.

God is not a mean and angry sky-dictator, waiting to strike vengeance upon those who make mistakes. God is looking for a reason to bless you, and, when you obey Him, you are cooperating with His efforts to put you in a good place.

Obedience toward God unlocks the favor of God. As you obey His instructions, you end up where you need to be, when you need to be there, with whom you need to be and in the proper conditions. Having God, the One Who knows the future and the intent of men's hearts, as your guide is highly advantageous. For the very One Who created you wants to lead you. When you obey, you walk along a safe path. When you are walking in obedience, you can be certain that everything that happens or doesn't happen to you is being used of God.

I cannot stress this law enough. Many believers are living in lack as a result of disobedience toward God. But the good news is that God is rich in more than one way, for He is rich in mercy. He is willing to move forward from this point and onward. In fact, every morning is a new opportunity to walk in the blessings of obedience.

"Great is his faithfulness; his mercies begin afresh each morning."
~ Lamentations 3:23

Here, I also want to stress that walking in disobedience can bring delay. And, while repentance is possible, time cannot be resurrected. But if you have been walking in disobedience, it won't do you any good either to let guilt and shame slow you down even further. Instead, jump on this moment now. Look at this instant as your fresh start. Though you've taken a thousand steps away from God, getting back to His plan never takes more than one single step of repentance. But act immediately.

As you are faithful to walk in obedience, a progressive repair will take place over your life and finances. Over time, the bad seeds will grow and die. And the good seeds will begin to grow in the coming seasons. The longer you walk in obedience, the more good seeds you get into the ground.

So where is the voice of God guiding you? In what ways are you committing financial disobedience? Identify it, own it, repent of it and next it. Move on. Begin taking steps of obedience today.

The Law of Obedience: obedience produces perfect position.

Having just become a pastor, I began recalling all of the times that I was disobedient. And, once having been a hardheaded disciple, I was then learning the pains of pastoring. Don't get me wrong. It's mostly a joy to pastor, but people can be vicious. I began to reminisce about the times I made things difficult for Pastor Johnny. I started to appreciate him in a whole new way. In fact, the first time he called me while I was in Hayward, I cried. With a newfound empathy for Pastor Johnny and tears in my eyes, I told him, "If I was a bad disciple, I'm sorry. If I did anything wrong, I'm sorry." Yet he comforted me over the phone.

And comfort couldn't come soon enough. My job search wasn't immediately fruitful, and money was starting to run out. However, I didn't panic. I trusted God.

Eventually, I landed a job at a Fiber Optics company to which I will refer to as "JCC". Though grateful, I noted the significant difference in my hourly rate. The telephone company in Ontario paid me $25 an hour. Now working at JCC, I was paid $9 an hour. It was a difference that left my family supported, but finances were tight.

At the time, JCC was contracted to do work at a very prestigious site – Stanford University. And, about a month into working at JCC, I was sent to do work at the University. And my goodness! The university left me awestruck.

The University seemed to spare no expense. The location was historically significant, financially extravagant and beautifully constructed. It looked like a little piece of Heaven on earth. I'm convinced that sometimes the world is keener to excellence than the church, though all excellence is reflective of Heavenly culture.

The trees were trim, the building materials were of the highest quality and the technology was cutting edge. I couldn't believe what I was seeing. The property was large, but everything was so well kept. I held such a high appreciation for being able to work at the University that every time I had a guest speaker come to my church, I would drive them to the campus and give them a grand tour. "This is where I work", I would enthusiastically explain. I felt such a stirring while on the property. I wouldn't know why until years later.

But after three months on the job, I received an $8 raise. Things were beginning to stabilize, and I was experiencing a season of joy. During all of this, of course, I stood faithful in sowing into our little church in Hayward.

Having completely thrown ourselves into the arms of God, we were experiencing the provision that comes from trusting in Him. We performed a trust fall, and God caught us.

Within the first six months, our church grew to about 100 members. And it was time for us to give a report about the church. We returned to Southern California for yet another church planting conference. This time, we went to share our story and update the fellowship.

#8 The Law of Greatness

And I was excited to give our church report, because Lori and I were experiencing church growth. Faithfulness was yielding its sweet fruit.

Faithfulness is the key to growth and expansion. Before God will give you much, He will first test you with little. If you're reading this book, you likely carry a passion within your heart to fund the gospel message and support the Kingdom of God. So you need to know this: Before God will bless you to where you can give out of abundance, He will first test you to see if you will give out of lack.

There are no short cuts in the Kingdom of God. Everything that God does takes both process and progress. He is a God of excellence and quality. Quality comes neither cheap nor quickly. God refines, crafts and perfects.

With God, promotion comes after a job well done, never before. The reason God requires faithfulness from us is because prosperity always comes with a purpose. In other words, God only considers the faithful as candidates. Faithfulness isn't a qualification for God's use and blessing. Faithfulness is the process by which God qualifies you.

You see, if God were to bring about blessing before its proper time, it would crush you. Faith is strength, and blessing is weight. Blessing is more of a responsibility than a reward.

"When someone has been given much, much will be required in return; and when someone has been entrusted with much, even more will be required."

~ **Luke 12:48**

So how does God reward us? He rewards us with Himself. God Himself is our reward. That's what He told to Abraham.

"After these things the word of the LORD came unto Abram in a vision, saying, Fear not, Abram: I *am* thy shield, *and* thy exceeding great reward."

~ **Genesis 15:1**

And though blessings are enjoyable, they are given to you for a purpose. And until you are ready to fulfill that certain purpose, God will not give that purpose's corresponding blessing. And your readiness is determined by your faithfulness.

But, even if you could, by means of force and trying, arrive at a place of blessing, you would not remain there very long if God didn't take you there Himself. So how do we avoid such hastiness? We simply must choose to act out of faith instead of frustration. Faith is trust in action, and faithfulness is the consistency of that trust over a considerable period of time. It takes time to have faithfulness.

So buckle down. Begin to think long-term. You can't have faithfulness in a few days, weeks or even months. Jesus didn't experience His most influential aspects of ministry until He was thirty. Moses spent forty years in a desert, and King David tended sheep.

But when it does arrive, God's blessing for faithfulness comes in a compounded and multiplied manner.

"For whoever has, to him more shall be given, and he will have an abundance; but whoever does not have, even what he has shall be taken away from him."

~ Matthew 13:12

So, when it comes to faithfulness, remember this: faithfulness shapes you and prepares you to fulfill a certain purpose. And that purpose comes with corresponding blessings. But those blessings are not just rewards. God is your reward. Rather, those blessings are the resources that you'll need to do what God has prepared you to do. Never forget that.

In essence, the reward for faithfulness is the honor of more to do. And in order to do that more, God provides you with resources. Faithfulness helps you to become that someone who can handle those resources. Certainly, we can also enjoy the blessings of God. We were created with the capability to enjoy life. But every blessing has an assignment. Those blessings will never precede God's preparation.

To help you fully appreciate why that is, consider lottery winners. Most lotto winners lose their cash prizes within a relatively short period of time. Why? It's because if you haven't developed the character, knowledge and mind to acquire greatness, you don't have the character, knowledge and mind to keep it. All the greats of God's Kingdom are faithful servants. Jesus said it best:

"He sat down, called the twelve disciples over to him, and said, 'Whoever wants to be first must take last place and be the servant of everyone else.'"

~ Mark 9:35

The Law of Greatness: A life of greatness is created in the daily acts of faithfulness.

As I wrote, because of the growth we were experiencing, I was eager to share my report. However, I had somewhat lost perspective. I thought that the results of my faithfulness were like badges of honor. But now I cringe when I remember the words I spoke at that conference. The time had come, and I approached the stage with a proud stride. I faced the crowd and opened my mouth. With a relaxed demeanor, I confidently shared, "You know, this is easy. I should have started a church much sooner." Lori recalls being in her seat thinking, "Yes, we should have done it sooner." We were both unscathed by the true tribulations of pastoring.

Also in the crowd were other pioneer pastors – some who were facing difficult times. In fact, many had been pastoring longer than I but had smaller churches. I should have been more sensitive and thoughtful with my approach. No matter now, for I was about to return to chaos.

After the conference, Lori and I returned to the church to find out that things weren't what they seemed. Gossip, a problem often hidden, had been tearing about at the church's foundation. By the time problems surfaced, it was too late. Having taken over a church, I was more like a stepdad than a father. The people we pastored had stayed, but their hearts were with the previous pastor. Though they still sat in our church chairs, the people were inwardly elsewhere.

People began an exodus. The church was crumbling before my eyes. Attendance was rapidly dropping. Lori and I got our taste of rejection, abandonment, resentment and anger. We had given our lives to help those people, so we wondered what was going on.

Here, I must admit that I was not a saint in handling the chaos. In fact, as I prepared my sermons, I would visualize specific individuals. My criticisms and insults of people were disguised as sermons points. It was my way of firing back. I was preaching about certain people and they knew it.

I know. That was not the best way to handle it. My need for growth was put on display for all to see. And, of course, as a result, the problem worsened. More people left the church. And many who stayed were in a state of bitterness and apathy. It was not a good scene.

Maybe this whole pastoring thing wasn't as "easy" as I had said it was. The season of dying had begun. It was winter in the spirit, and hearts were cold. But in the middle of a very dark season, a seed of hope was planted.

#9 The Law of Persistence

We all face difficult times. But only those who endure will ever see the fruit of persistence. In fact, you haven't ever really failed until you've given up. While faithfulness is faith over time, persistence is the will to be faithful. Persistence is an internal state of being. It is also consistent, determined, concentrated activity. There is a certain focus to persistence. Persistence is not a broad expense of effort. It is a very specific series of consistent actions.

"Keep on asking, and you will receive what you ask for. Keep on seeking, and you will find. Keep on knocking, and the door will be opened to you."

~ Matthew 7:7

Ask God. If He doesn't seem to answer, get up and go seek Him. And if, when you arrive at His door, you find that He doesn't seem to be home, keep knocking. Ask, seek and knock.

"So let's not get tired of doing what is good. At just the right time we will reap a harvest of blessing if we don't give up."

~ Galatians 6:9

If you keep going, victory is guaranteed. If you persist, you eventually win. Feel like quitting? Good! Persistence doesn't even start until you feel like you've got nothing left. Almost every success story begins as a nightmare of non-stop failures.

Is there something you believe will eventually happen? Are you expecting a breakthrough in your business, your ministry, your family, your relationships or your spirituality? Have you gone through New Year after New Year, telling yourself, "This is my year" with seemingly no results? Good. How bad do you want it? How long are you willing to wait? And, for that matter, how do you know that you're not half way there? Almost there? Who knows what can happen in the next twenty-four hours but God? How do you know that you're not a day away from breakthrough? A week away? How many people do you think gave up within only days of their breakthrough and don't even know it? Have you heard all this before? Good. Every disappointment brings you closer to appointment. Every disillusionment makes you a better candidate for a miracle. God wants nobody else to take credit for what only He can do. You've persisted this long. So if you quit now, what has become of all your waiting? Persist, and you will win. You're not an exception to the law of persistence.

The Law of Persistence: If you keep going, you will eventually reach your destination – no exceptions.

I persisted despite my dark season. Six more months had gone by, and, for those six months, the church continued to fall apart. But it was time for another church planting conference. This time, I attended the conference with my head held low. I was humbled and war-wearied.

There was a morning session taking place, and the president of the fellowship, Pastor Mike Neville, was ministering. He was

71

teaching on paradigm shifts and breaking old mentalities. One such mentality that needed to break was our fellowship's attitude toward money. Praise Chapel never really emphasized any teaching on finance. Now, there's nothing wrong with that in it of itself. The fellowship has its own dynamic DNA. But every movement has need of growth in one place or another.

While ministering on the changing of mindsets, seeming to be prophetically aware of this need for growth, Pastor Neville addressed the fellowship's lack of perspective on finances. What was about to happen was pivotal in my life.

If ever God has spoken to you at a church service, it can seem as though He has singled you out. Actually, I can recall this happening to me quite a bit. In my early years of Christianity, I often accused my brother Alfred of informing the preachers about me. The Holy Spirit often spoke directly to my heart through anointed men. It was as if their sermons were prepared just for me. It happened often enough that, eventually, I stopped accusing my brother of feeding the preachers information about my life.

And this time, the Holy Spirit would use Mike Neville to impart a seed, a dream and a vision. There were about a thousand people in the room, but I feel, to this day, as though God singled me out. I felt like that moment was a gift from God. While ministering on the rare topic of finances, Mike Neville stopped in the middle of his message. The atmosphere shifted, as he began to prophesy. There seemed to be currents of electricity in the air.

"God just spoke to me", he said. A hush came over the room. "There are future millionaires in this place. Who are you?" As soon as he spoke those words, something lit up within me. Inspiration surged through my entire being. My heart raced, and my soul leaped. I don't know how, but I knew it was me. Then God spoke.

I heard in my spirit, "You. It's you." I looked at my wife and said, "Lori, that's us." Puzzled, she inquired, "Are you sure?" My response was resolute: "Yes, I heard God tell me that it's me."

Just then, Mike Neville further instructed, "If that's you, I want to challenge you to stand to your feet. We're going to pray." So, with hearts filled with faith, Lori and I stood up. I had no idea how that would ever come about. After all, I was the pastor of a small, crumbling church and a manual laborer at a Fiber Optics company.

I couldn't imagine how things would become good again let alone great. But in our darkest moments, God imparts the most unusual and unlikely dreams.

#10 The Law of Declaration

I said, "Lori, that's us!" I opened my mouth and declared the dream. Now, I know that life isn't as simple as speaking what you want. But there is certainly a power behind speech. For your words can both cause things to change and reveal your heart's current state. Words carry power.

"The tongue can bring death or life; those who love to talk will reap the consequences."

~ Proverbs 18:21

You were created in the image of God. Your Father is the Creator of the universe. And I believe that some of His powers of creative speech have been passed along to you. Of course, our creativity isn't as powerful as God's creativity. But your words still carry weight. They can cause harm or help.

Even Jesus spoke of this amazing ability when teaching us about prayer:

"Then Jesus said to the disciples, "Have faith in God. I tell you the truth, you can say to this mountain, 'May you be lifted up and thrown into the sea,' and it will happen. But you must really believe it will happen and have no doubt in your heart. I tell you, you can pray for anything, and if you believe that you've received it, it will be yours."
~ Mark 11:22-24

Speaking life is important, but, especially if you're prone to negativity, it can be difficult to make positive speech a lasting habit. Allow your mind to act as a filter for your words. And let that filter be calibrated by God's Word. Allow your words to become positive over time. This has both a practical and supernatural effect.

Practically, positive speech surrounds you with positive people, can open opportunities for you, can build important connections for you and give your Christianity a good name. Supernaturally, it can influence the spiritual climate that you carry with you and create realities.

When it comes to your speech, this is a good rule or question of measurement: would you want it to come true? Does what you say align with what you want? If your words had the same level of creativity as God's, what sort of world would you be creating for yourself? Declare truth. Declare the dream. Believe in the awesome power of declaration.

The Law of Declaration: Words create atmospheres and influence reality.

After the conference, Lori and I returned to our battlefront. I want to tell you that we then experienced revival. I want to tell you that we never again doubted God. I want to tell you that we never once questioned the dream. But that wouldn't be true. Not only would I be lying, but I would also be robbing you. You see, I want you to know that the blessing of prosperity is a journey, not a destination. Before new levels, there will always come greater tests, trials and resistance. God will not bless one who He has yet to test. Faith is strengthened under resistance.

When we returned to Hayward, things got even worse. The weariness began to weigh on me. I had to care for a marriage, a family, a church and a full-time job. I even continued to go on mission trips, as well as fund our little church. I continued along the path of self-denial, hard work and rugged faithfulness.

To be honest with you, I even eventually forgot about the dream that was imparted to me at the conference. The dream being that I was called to be a millionaire. We kept trying to build, but there was no breakthrough, no refreshing.

We continued in the muck of resistance for about a year.

In fact, we even became slightly disgruntled. I had to make a real strong effort to guard my heart against bitterness and frustration. Trials without become most damaging when they become trials within. So I stood close to the Lord, and only He was able to guard my heart.

I also grew frustrated toward pastor Johnny Dorris. I was under the impression that it was his job to check up on me. Because I rarely heard from him, I admit, it got to me. I even considered leaving the church!

In fact, an "opportunity" came my way. Another church fellowship was looking to hire a full-time pastor. Lori and I went in to interview for the position, and it looked like a wonderful opportunity. The church had a building, wonderful people and a comfortable salary. I imagined what it would be like to pastor full-time without the time-consumption of a full-time job. It was, to me, an ideal offer. I thought for sure that it was God's open door to us.

The pastor who interviewed us was enthusiastic about Lori and I. But then he spoke words that pricked my heart. "Wow! You know I would love to have you guys join us right now. But I want you to do something. I want you to go home and pray."

He didn't just burst my bubble. He knocked the wind out of me. Sure enough, God spoke a resounding, "No." God wanted me to stay with Praise Chapel. To be honest, I suspected that all along. Remembering my commitment, I said, "Yes" to God. Lori and I had to be honest with ourselves about where God wanted us.

#11 The Law of Honesty

Prosperity isn't just about where you go but also about how you arrived there. Is the journey just as godly as the destination? It is important to be honest to both yourself and others. Dishonesty creates the illusion of success, entices you with gratification and keeps you from becoming someone who can be truly successful.

"Dishonest money dwindles away, but whoever gathers money little by little makes it grow."

~ Proverbs 13:11

Honesty goes a long way when it comes to prosperity. Too many gain finances by being dishonest with themselves or with other people. But can a dishonest person ever truly be considered prosperous?

I often tell my disciples to stay clean. Even if it seems as though you're getting away with something, if you continue in dishonest ways, you will be caught. How would one be able to enjoy wealth gained dishonestly? They would live in the constant fear of being exposed. Keep your conscience clean, your God happy and your foundation firm. Dishonest gain is just a sand castle in the path of a wave. It'll be gone any second.

How do you handle your business dealings? How do you deal with your finances? Are you deceptive with customers, the government or your employees? How do you handle your ministry or relationships? Honestly ask yourself if you're being truly honest.

The Law of Honesty: If a man is not honest, he can never be prosperous.

Over time, I saw Christ developing in my character. God was doing something through the difficult times. He does not waste the difficult times of our lives.

Then, the monotony was broken by an unusual invitation. Lori and I were invited to a conference. No, it wasn't a Praise Chapel church-planting conference. This one was different.

It was held in Portland, Oregon and on the topic of Biblical Prosperity. Recalling the prophetic words of Mike Neville, I became quite interested in the conference. Thankfully, the friend who invited us also offered to sponsor us.

Being completely candid, I admit that I would have taken any trip that took me out of Hayward. Any time away seemed like a vacation. Needless to say, we went to the conference.

The speaker lineup was amazing: Larry Huch, Creflo Dollar, E.V. Hill, John Avanzini – all gifted in ministering Biblical prosperity. The sessions were life transforming. The speakers addressed prosperity, finances, generosity, money, business and the like. I was like a dry sponge, and every word they spoke was moist refreshment.

But my greatest breakthrough came in the quietness of a prayer room. Before each main session, the conference hosted an open prayer gathering. The purpose of the gatherings was to cultivate a time in which conference attendees could process all they were receiving throughout the week. And I certainly had a lot to process.

As I was seeking the Lord in prayer and meditating on all that I had heard, God spoke to my heart: "When you return to Hayward, you're going to lose even more people."

"What on earth? I came here for a breakthrough. How is that supposed to help me?" I thought to myself. God continued, "And you're not going to be a millionaire. You're going to be a multimillionaire." God's words brought about mixed feelings, but peace had calmed me to settle in faith.

That same night, after the service, a dinner was held for the conference attendees. While enjoying our time there, Lori and I were approached by John Avanzini himself. It was an honor. Upon approaching our table, Mr. Avanzini greeted us and then spoke, "Share with me about your life. What do you do?"

I poured out my heart to him. I explained everything – my testimony, my pioneer mission, my church, my job and my family. Upon hearing my story, Mr. Avanzini called for his assistant to approach the table. Mr. Avanzini instructed his assistant, "Go to my table and grab some books." The assistant came back with 2 bags filled with books. The book topics varied within a niche – faith, prosperity, money, and public speaking. They were a free gift – to me from John Avanzini. He even signed some of the books.

Lori and I were refreshed. It was time to go home. A fresh sense of duty was bestowed upon us. Sure enough, the word of the Lord came to pass. Well, at least, the *first* portion of the word came to pass.

People began to leave our already shrinking church. Within a week, we lost about one-third of our church – members, leaders and volunteers. Though somewhat scathed, my faith remained intact. We were thankful for those who stayed, even though most of the ones who stayed were none tithe-payers. Yes, mostly all of my tithe-paying members had left, but the bills stood faithful – almost $5,000 worth of monthly expenses.

In the middle of it all, I recognized the chaos for what it truly was: it was a test from God. Would I trust God for provision? Would I remember that He owns it all?

Lori and I felt every emotion you can think of, but our faith stood rooted in God's promises. His promises are a sure foundation. We decided, we determined to put God to the test.

He promised us that we were going to be multi-millionaires. I didn't ask for it. I never even thought myself to be capable of it. But it was His promise and His will. So He was the only one who could bring it about. Looking at us then, most would not consider us to have a bright future. We were in the middle of a storm – the storm had lasted for years. But the dream in my heart marked a new beginning of a new season. Something good was going to happen. I just knew it.

I took the books that John Avanzini had given to me, and I made the time to read them. I was pastoring a church, caring for a family and working full-time. But I made the time to read the books. I considered it an investment. Of course, I also stood faithful to my personal prayer devotion and study of God's Word. I began to walk out the Biblical principles of prosperity:

Speak it…

Walk in faith…

Understand that God is the Provider…

One Sunday morning, shortly after our major church member exodus, Lori gave me the news that the church was short about

$1,300 that month. And it was the last Sunday of the month. We had one service to come up with $1,300, and the average church offering rarely ever broke beyond $200.

That morning, when I arrived at the church, my mind was assessing the situation. I planned and mapped how we might come up with such an amount. I was stressed. I felt a knot in the pit of my stomach.

You've been there. Maybe you're there right now. It can seem like a dark cloud is hovering just above your head, like you're trapped in a small space.

Anyway, I went to my office and got to thinking. Suddenly, I felt as though I found an appropriate solution. "Pledges!" I said to myself, "I'll take pledges. If each person commits to a certain amount, I can raise the money."

What a great idea! Confident, I stood up from my chair and approached the door. I was already rehearsing how I might present the pledge drive to the church. But just as quickly as the thought came, God struck it down. The Lord sternly rebuked me: "I'm not broke! You are! Get out there and tell the people that I own it all. Tell them that every need will be met."

I bargained with the Lord for only a minute or two. How can one argue with God? Apprehensive but intent on obeying, I approached the pulpit. After the worship and preliminaries, it was time for offering. I couldn't believe what I was hearing myself say. "God owns it all. Everything is going to be taken care of. We are blessed."

I continued with such declarations for about ten minutes. I didn't pull or pry. I just declared the faithfulness of God. I shared of His ability to take care of our needs. And I told the church that God has everything that we need. I even went as far as declaring that all of the church's needs were going to be met, that there was nothing to cause concern.

After the service, I approached Lori, who, at the time, counted the offerings. I asked to know the amount that had been received in the offering.

The result?

$1,500 came in that one service. God had met the need and then some. But God didn't stop there.

One year passed. And in the one year that it took to rebuild the church, not a single bill ever went without being paid. Every need was met.

And beyond.

We were experiencing the provision of God. Little did we know, God was barely getting started.

#12 The Law of the Word

The Word of God delivered me from my financial bind, and it can do the same for you.

"Study this Book of Instruction continually. Meditate on it day and night so you will be sure to obey everything written in it. Only then will you prosper and succeed in all you do."

~ Joshua 1:8

If we do not conduct ourselves according to the Word of God, we will not prosper. And if we don't read the Word, we will not know how to conduct ourselves.

There are over 2,000 verses about money in the Bible, and 15% of Jesus' Biblically recorded teachings are about money. The Bible has much to say about prosperity, business, money, generosity, wisdom and wealth.

If you will base what you do on the Word of God, you will become prosperous. The one who meditates on the Word of God flourishes and becomes strong.

**"How blessed is the man
who does not walk in the counsel of the wicked,
Nor stand in the path of sinners,
Nor sit in the seat of scoffers!
But his delight is in the law of the LORD,
And in His law he meditates day and night.
He will be like a tree *firmly* planted by streams of water,
Which yields its fruit in its season
And its leaf does not wither;
And in whatever he does, he prospers."**

~ Psalm 1:1-3

If we are to be considered servants of God, we must let our Master's instruction touch every aspect of our lives. We cannot compartmentalize God's influence. Let Him influence your money and business. Allow the power of the Word of God to bring about change and freedom.

Do you consider the Word of God in your business activity and plans? Does the Truth of the Bible have any influence on your money?

The Law of the Word: If prosperity is a destination then the Bible is the map.

Chapter 5
Small Beginnings

I was thankful for what God was doing in my life, but I knew there was much more that He had for me. God withholds from us until we grow. He will not bless us beyond our level of faith. If we don't have the faith to receive it, we definitely don't yet have the character to keep it. But sometimes, while we are waiting on God, we can forget that God is waiting on us.

"The LORD will send rain at the proper time from his rich treasury in the heavens and will bless all the work you do. You will lend to many nations, but you will never need to borrow from them."

~ Deuteronomy 28:12

The *work* of our hands – not our hands – is blessed. Faith doesn't sit idly. Faith is trust in action. Faith is hard work. Faith is even sometimes the taking of a risk. If there is no risk, there is no reward. And if there is no risk, faith is not required. Many shy away from risk, while claiming to be wise. But we must realize that risk and wisdom are not always at odds with one another.

The difference between those who prosper and those who do not – the defining difference – is how they respond to fear, how they respond to risk. Those who have prospered were willing to take risks, while those who live in poverty fearfully shy away from risk.

Risk is the appropriate response of faith. But what is the difference between foolishness and faith? Where do we draw the line on risk and reward? The only difference between faith and foolishness is whether or not God has spoken. If you respond to God's leading, it's faith. If you respond to your own assumptions, it's foolishness. God's voice is the distinguishing factor. He is no fool who obeys God.

We go from glory to glory. God will not ask something of you that your faith is not ready to handle. He steadily raises the challenge. Each new challenge will always seem just a little above our ability to reach. In fact, the growth of our faith is so progressive that we often fail to see the growth that is taking place within us.

There are steps of faith, and then there are leaps of faith, defining moments in our walk with God. For those times, God gives us a gift of faith (**1 Corinthians 12:9**).

And so I was about to take another step of faith on the stairway of my destiny. Working at JCC, I gained some experience in telecommunications, but I was by no means an expert. Still, I knew enough to begin picking up some work on the side.

#13 The Law of Wisdom

Prosperity comes in proportion to wisdom. Wisdom is the ability to effectively apply knowledge. It is not just knowing what to do but also when to do it, how to do it, with whom to do it and so on. The book of proverbs records some powerful words, words spoken by wisdom herself.

"Common sense and success belong to me.
Insight and strength are mine.
Because of me, kings reign,
and rulers make just decrees.
Rulers lead with my help,
and nobles make righteous judgments.
I love all who love me.
Those who search will surely find me.
I have riches and honor,
as well as enduring wealth and justice.
My gifts are better than gold, even the purest gold,
my wages better than sterling silver!
I walk in righteousness,
in paths of justice.
Those who love me inherit wealth.
I will fill their treasuries.
The Lord formed me from the beginning,
before he created anything else."
~ Proverbs 8:14-22

Remember that prosperity is more than just wealth or financial stability. There is a certain wholeness factor to prosperity that touches all aspects of life. You can gain wealth with only knowledge, but you cannot have prosperity without wisdom. In fact, it was because of Solomon's request for wisdom that God saw him fit to receive the manifold benefits of prosperity.

"God said to Solomon, 'Because your greatest desire is to help your people, and you did not ask for wealth, riches, fame, or even the death of your enemies or a long life, but rather you asked for wisdom and knowledge to properly govern my people— I will certainly give you the wisdom and knowledge you requested. But I will also give you wealth, riches, and fame such as no other king has had before you or will ever have in the future!'"

~ 2 Chronicles 1:11-12

Wisdom is the proper application of knowledge. It is both sound and centered judgment. It is calculating and predictive, time-saving and efficient. If anyone feels that they lack this divine sense of reasoning, they can approach God for it.

"If you need wisdom, ask our generous God, and he will give it to you. He will not rebuke you for asking."

~ James 1:5

Are you wise in your handling of money? Do your actions on the job make you look wise or foolish? If God were to bless you with everything you are asking of Him, could you handle it?

The Law of Wisdom: Prosperity is given in proportion to wisdom.

In 1992, I started a side business, *Paul's Phone Service*. In addition to providing basic telecommunication services, I also picked up scraps of cables, copper and such. As Lori will tell you, I had no business location. So we had to strip the wires in our living room.

During this time, our church was doing good, but my personal finances needed a boost. Our kids were growing into teenagers. And, as any parent will tell you, teenagers are more expensive than kids. Also, the church had stopped paying our housing allowance and various other expenses.

So Lori made a flyer, and my son, Paulie, distributed the flyers around the neighborhood. The flyer advertised my work. I installed telephone lines, jacks and fax lines. Hundreds of flyers made their way all around town.

Yet not a single customer called.

Still, it was nice having my family contribute their time to the business. I determined to stay encouraged. Eventually, we placed a $48 advertisement in the penny saver. The ad ran for 8 weeks.

Our faith and persistence was met by God's blessing. People began to call. That first year, we made a decent profit. The profits almost doubled consecutively.

The first year, we profited $13,000
The second year, we profited $44,600
The third year, we profited $70,000

I was beginning to see the hand of God at work in the business. He was faithful to His Word.

#14 The Law of Reciprocity

What you give comes back to you multiplied. That is the law of reciprocity.

"Give, and you will receive. Your gift will return to you in full--pressed down, shaken together to make room for more, running over, and poured into your lap. The amount you give will determine the amount you get back."

~ Luke 6:38

You and God participate together in a life of exchange. You gave him your life, because He gave you His. You give Him your faith, and He gives you His power. You give Him glory, and He shows you His Glory.

God entrusts you with earthly and spiritual resources. Your time, talent and treasures are all yours to invest. You are to invest those in life and multiply their value. Of course, God requires the firsts of each. And with those firsts, God makes investments of His own. And from that, He blesses you. And when He blesses you, you have more to invest. So then the firsts, that you are to give to God, become larger. The longer this exchange continues, the greater the effect of multiplication.

God measures how He will bless you in accordance with how you bless others and the gospel. And when you sow into the gospel, it's as if you're putting investments into the very hand of God. And Who better is there to multiply your investment? When we give, we are making Heavenly investments. It's almost as if we're buying stock in Heaven.

"Store your treasures in heaven, where moths and rust cannot destroy, and thieves do not break in and steal."
~ Matthew 6:20

If you read my book's introduction, you'll recall that Paul told Timothy that his earthly treasure could be invested with Heavenly gain.

"...each those who are rich in this world not to be proud and not to trust in their money, which is so unreliable. Their trust should be in God, who richly gives us all we need for our

enjoyment. Tell them to use their money to do good. They should be rich in good works and generous to those in need, always being ready to share with others. By doing this they will be storing up their treasure as a good foundation for the future so that they may experience true life."

~ 1 Timothy 6:17-19

Money is important, but it is based upon an earthly system. I'm not trying to be negative, but the truth is that our economy could collapse. Our dollars are only as secure as our economy. But when you invest in the Kingdom of God, you are investing in an everlasting, indestructible and Heavenly economy. When you sow into the gospel, you are making a divine investment, backed by God's credibility.

And Heavenly currency is much more valuable. So when God returns some of your Heavenly investment, the exchange rate favors you. Giving to God is like setting a pendulum into motion. The back-and-forth swings become stronger and higher.

Are you participating in a lifestyle of exchange with God? Do you trust an earthly system more than a Heavenly one? If you're not willing to exchange with God, you are avoiding the acceleration of prosperity.

The Law of Reciprocity: God gives returns on your Heavenly investments.

Our fourth year in business was our seventh year in Hayward. Seven is God's number of maturity and completion. I knew it was time to turn my side business into a full-time business. I left JCC and went full-time into my own business.

91

Eventually, I landed a contract with a familiar customer. Leave it to God to bless me in such a poetic fashion. He's a good God.

Stanford University.

Once an employee working there, I had become a business owner doing contract work there. I was completely ethical and never worked against JCC. But I can't help but think of this verse:

"If you listen to these commands of the LORD your God that I am giving you today, and if you carefully obey them, the LORD will make you the head and not the tail, and you will always be on top and never at the bottom."

~ Deuteronomy 28:13

But I soon lost perspective. Excited and living in the blessing of God, I let my guard down. A desperate man will seek God on every matter. A blessed man is not so keen to do the same. Taking on Stanford University as a client, I felt overwhelmed. Without prayerful consideration, I entered into a partnership that I thought would help to carry the load. It would turn out to be an important lesson learned.

For the sake of my former partner's privacy, I will refer to him as "Gary". My agreement with Gary was as follows: he would take care of the administrative aspects of the business, and I would handle the service aspect of the business. Gary had the licensing for bigger jobs, and I had the contacts. He handled structure. I handled the jobs.

Our partnership seemed to work at first. We were even able to hire several members of my church.

But Gary soon proved to be unorganized and very secretive. I trusted him, so I never even saw the company books or financial records. I had believed that he was handling finances and organization properly. But a sense of uneasiness slowly crept over me.

Now you must understand that I hold nothing against Gary. I share this story only because it was an important part of my journey, though a rough part.

I am very meticulous when it comes to work. I like people being on time. I like hard workers. I like transparency. And I highly value consistency. But it gradually became apparent to me that Gary wasn't going to keep up with his end of the business. Incomplete jobs, lazy responses to pressing work demands and an overall apathetic approach – that was Gary's style. And not only was it worrying me. It was frustrating me to the max. He would drop the ball on quotes and failed to provide the administrative assistance that I needed to complete jobs in a timely manner. Tension began to build between Gary and I.

Now Gary had a group of friends who so happened to be lawyers. As he would vent to them about our tense partnership, they would plant ideas in his head. They told him that he was the sole owner of the company and that I was just a laborer. Rejecting our 50/50 partnership, Gary began to see me as unimportant and easily replaced.

Now for the difficult part…

My agreement with Gary was a *verbal* agreement. We didn't sign a written, contractual agreement. We were friends, so at the start that didn't seem necessary. In fact, I was his pastor. He was a disciple in my church. So when it came down to it, I didn't have a whole lot of backing when he started to deny my being his equal partner.

Now remember, I was hiring people from my church. I knew that if things got worse between Gary and I, jobs would be put at risk. Fallout was the last thing I wanted. I tried to patch things up between us. But the entangling between my work and Gary's work was bringing us both down. Before I could begin the process of change and improvement, Gary came after me. He wanted everything, the whole company.

He wanted my contacts, my workers and my supplies. Also, recall that Gary was the one with the licensing for bigger jobs. Gary had, without my knowledge, removed my name from everything at the very start. He was very shrewd. But I knew I had to break away or I would disappoint both my employees and clients.

Was I to stay and make things work? Or was I to take the loss and start afresh? It was a dilemma. I took the matter to prayer.

During this time, I had a very prophetic guest speaker come to the church. His name was Robert Sanchez. I have come to fondly refer to him as "The Sanchez". Rob knew absolutely nothing about what was going on with my business, but he gave me a very bizarre word. Rob said, "When your partner says, 'You make me so mad that I want to bite your hand', it's time to split the partnership."

Very odd indeed. But sure enough, during one of our regular disputes, Gary got angry and told me, "You make me so mad that I want to bite your hand!" I was stunned at the prophetic accuracy of the Sanchez. But I also knew it was time to split.

In the end, I made a swift breakaway, but Gary took the company.

#15 The Law of Good Company

Gary wasn't an evil man. He wasn't a demonic man. And Gary wasn't a criminal. However, Gary was not a divine connection.

"Can two people walk together without agreeing on the direction?"

~ Amos 3:3

Relationships are like ropes. If you're roped to someone who isn't heading in the same direction as you, you cannot continue to move. You'll be stuck in the struggle of resistance and conflict. You cannot accomplish success with someone who has a different definition of success than you do. I'm not saying that we shouldn't have friends who disagree with us. I'm just saying that the closer you're tied together, the more similar your direction should be.

So bad fits can be considered bad company. And bad company will destroy you.

"Don't be fooled by those who say such things, for 'bad company corrupts good character.'"

~ 1 Corinthians 15:33

Is there an Achan in your camp? Is there a Jonah on board your boat? Could it be that some of the people with whom you've connected are blocking the blessing of prosperity?

The Law of Good Company: Good company accelerates your pace toward prosperity, and bad company does the opposite.

That was a tough lesson learned. Moving forward, I started from almost zero. I had workers but no supplies. I pressed forward, resolving to never again be hasty about business decisions. After all, it was God's business, not mine.

But how to start again? The only thing more discouraging than a desperate situation is a desperate situation that comes *after* a time of great success.

Pimentel Communications.

That was the name of my business, then rechristened. We even got our own license so no partnership would be necessary. We were off to a slow start, but I stood faithful to the Biblical principles of business. We picked up jobs here and there. At the time, we had only about $10,000 in the business account, yet I was feeling good about the fresh start. But I was praying for a large contract, one that would launch us back into steady business.

Soon, my prayers were answered. I was offered a contract from another University – a $200,000 contract. It was a contract that would have helped to regain my company's stride. But nothing grand comes without persistent faith. There was one issue: I had no credit line, and I needed material to complete the job.

In the midst of this situation, it was time again to return to Southern California for yet another church planting conference. It was a nice refresher, but I was unable to attend the conference in its entirety. One of the conference sessions fell on the same day as a very important meeting that I had arranged. So, on that particular day, Lori went to the conference without me.

I had set up a meeting with the suppliers. The business was in need, and I was hoping that they would extend to me the needed credit. As the old saying goes, "It takes money to make money."

Without the credit, there was no extra money. Without the extra money, I had no supplies. Without the supplies, I couldn't start the contract. Without the contract, I couldn't get my company's momentum back. I had much relying on the suppliers approving the credit. So, as you might imagine, the meeting's atmosphere had a slight tension to it – tension similar to the uneasiness one might feel at a medical appointment.

At the meeting with the suppliers, I presented to them my proposal. As I presented, two very sharply dressed businesswomen sat across from me on the other end of a very long table. While I was making my request, the two women just quietly stared at me – they carried very serious demeanors. To be honest, it was intense. The atmosphere was somber, as one would expect of a business meeting. My voice carried in the quietness of the small conference room. Yet all along, I kept a faith-filled anticipation. I was expecting God to grant me favor. The stale air around me couldn't shake my faith. Still, I couldn't help but wonder what their response would exactly be. I put all that I had into that presentation and proposed a solid plan.

After my presentation, one of the women finally spoke. Time seemed to slow down, as I intently listened to the words that were carried by her soft-spoken voice. "Mr. Pimentel, we know who you are. We know the great work that you've done in the past. We remember you from your former company. The problem is that, on paper, there is nothing legal that lists you as an owner of your former company. You have to understand. We can only go by what's on paper. Because you're not listed as a former owner, we cannot extend to you the same credit that we have before extended to you. Unfortunately, it doesn't look like we can offer you the credit at this time."

At first discouraged, I eventually mustered the persistent faith to politely press the issue. After about another forty-five minutes of long discussion and discourse, one of the women asked me, "Mr. Pimentel, other than running this company, what do you do?" I told them, "I'm a pastor." After I elaborated on my pastoral experience and goals, they huddled together and began to whisper to each other.

Waiting in my seat across such a long table, I could only guess at what they were saying to each other. Whispering to one another and occasionally glancing back at me, they talked among themselves. Were they annoyed with me? Did they want to help? I know they saw the eagerness in my eyes, and I know they took note of my persistent approach.

What were they going to do?

Meanwhile, down at the church planting conference in Southern California, unknown to me, Lori was attending a special day session. And, in between sessions, she was speaking with a pastor during one of the breaks. The pastor, a trusted and known friend, told Lori about a financial need that one of his missionaries had. In order for him to effectively continue and expand his missionary work in a very harsh Russian environment, the missionary was in need of a vehicle. The pastor went on to explain that the vehicle would cost around $2,500. Lori, recalling that there was $10,000 in our bank account, told the pastor, "We will buy it for you." The pastor responded with gratitude, grateful that his Russian missionary would be well equipped to continue his work.

Looking back now, Lori and I can pinpoint the very minute of our separate experiences. At the very same moment that Lori was sowing, I was sweating and awaiting a response from my suppliers. I believe – I know in my spirit – that the financial seed my wife sowed on our behalf had unlocked the favor of God. That seed was sown in the very same moment that I was awaiting a response.

I believe that, because back at the meeting with the suppliers, at that same moment, one of the women spoke up, "Mr. Pimentel, we're going to up your credit line, because you're a pastor."

The business was reborn by *supernatural* means.

#16 The Law of Generosity

Wealth without generosity is still poverty. Generosity is an exercise in divinity. God is generous: He gave you life, salvation, hope, His Son and Heaven too. If you are not generous, there lacks in you something of Christ's character. If you are not generous, you are not truly prosperous. You don't have to be a millionaire to be prosperous. But you do have to be whole. And part of being whole is possessing the quality of generosity.

"The generous will prosper; those who refresh others will themselves be refreshed."

~ Proverbs 11:25

Being generous takes faith. Being generous also takes obedience toward God. Generosity isn't an amount; it's an attitude. It's possible to give a large amount and lack generosity. It's all relative to where you are in finance, influence, success and resources.

Why do some think that God would financially bless someone who doesn't demonstrate generosity? What reason would He have for putting finances into their hands? If God's decision to financially bless you was based solely upon your level of generosity, would He do it?

The Law of Generosity: the generous will prosper.

Chapter 6
More Tests

After securing the needed credit, my company and I got right to work. We didn't waste a single resource or moment. I have learned that God will bless you. And depending upon how you handle His blessing, He may bless you again.

My employees and I worked hard on that first big job. And the favor of God became even more apparent, as we completed a job that should have taken 2 months in 10 days.

That one job propelled Pimentel Communications into the future.

And momentum began to build over the next three years. Though there were no large company growth spurts, we did experience a steady growth over that period of time.

But it was right in the middle of growth that I was again tested.

#17 The Law of Contentment

What you're about to read is a story of grave warning. It is a lesson in the danger of not being content. But before you go on to read the story, I want to write to you about the law of contentment.

I was thankful for what God was doing in my company, but that doesn't mean that I didn't pursue more. Gratitude is an attitude not an action. So it's possible to thank God and ask God at the same time.

"Don't worry about anything; instead, pray about everything. Tell God what you need, and thank him for all he has done."

~ Philippians 4:6

You can tell God what you need, while thanking Him for all He has done. But it is important to be gracious and appreciative.

"*Let your* conversation *be* without covetousness; *and be* content with such things as ye have: for he hath said, I will never leave thee, nor forsake thee."

~ Hebrews 13:5

God has given us Himself. What more is there really? Entitlement is a mark of poverty. When you become angry at God for what you don't have, you prevent God from blessing you. When you look at the blessings of others and become jealous instead of inspired, you are not following the law of contentment.

Do you truly appreciate what you have? Do you want more for the sake of competition or for the sake of the great commission? If your children treated what you give to them the way you treat what God has given you, would you give them more? When you are content, you show God that blessings have not become an addiction. You demonstrate that He remains the apple of your eye. And when He is your delight, all things are in order for you to receive.

"Delight yourself in the LORD, and he will give you the desires of your heart."

~ Psalm 37:4

The Law of Contentment: appreciating what you have shows God that you can handle more.

On with the story...

A lack of contentment had led someone close to me to sin against me, and my son discovered the transgression.

It was in this season that God had positioned my son Paulie as a strategic part of Pimentel Communications.

Working as a project lead at the time, my son made a stop at the office to verify the payroll. He had never before looked at the payroll books in detail, but he had grown suspicious that some of our site workers were claiming more hours than they had actually worked. He was checking over the books to see if our workers' time sheets were matching up with what we were paying them. He not only found that several workers had given themselves extra hours, but he also discovered something that surprised him even more.

He noticed that the office manager, a key company employee, had been paid a much larger amount than Paulie knew. Thinking that I had approved the pay raise, Paulie assumed that I was just being generous, as I had always taught him to be.

When Paulie had discovered the supposed raise, I was in the Philippines on a missionary trip. Unhappy about what he thought he had uncovered, Paulie wanted to express his disagreement with my paying the office manager so much more than originally agreed. However, anyone who works with me knows to not call me while I am abroad. There's nothing I can do about most issues while overseas, so I'd rather not carry the stress without an ability to do anything about it. And so it happened that Paulie waited for my return to the States to confront me.

It would be a week before my return. But once back at the office, I was approached by my son. Paulie reported to me that everything at Pimentel Communications was in great shape, save for a few typical business-related problems and the matter of the raise. Paulie, feeling uneasy about the manager's pay, spoke candidly to me, "I can't believe how much of a raise you gave to our office manager."

Knowing that I had, in fact, given our office manager a reasonable raise, I retorted, "Well, Paulie, that aspect of the business doesn't really concern you. What I do with the money is up to me." Insistent that the amount was way too much, Paulie maintained, "Yes, but you gave him an extra $1,000 per check."

Knowing that I had approved no such amount, I fired back, "No!" Paulie asserted, "Well, that's what the books say - $1,000 a check." Upon hearing this, I had hoped it was a discrepancy in the books or that perhaps Paulie was not properly calculating the amounts. But my son is excellent with numbers, and I intuitively knew that it was something worse, though I didn't wish to believe that at the moment.

Nevertheless, Paulie showed me the books. I was stunned and hurt. In fact, the office manager had given himself an extra $1,000 per check. And he had been doing so for about a year. The office manager had complete control of the office, so nobody else ever saw or needed to see the payroll books. Because of our trust for him, the office manager knew that it was easy money. It wasn't likely that he would have ever been caught had Paulie not looked at the books himself.

Once I was caught up to speed, I was encouraged by Paulie to take immediate action. He said, "Let's get him in here and confront him." My son is very protective of me, and I know that he was just as upset as I was. But I wanted to take the matter to prayer and confront it properly. I knew that I had to confront the man who was stealing from me, but, first, I needed to pray. I also wanted to make sure that HR was involved. So, over the next three weeks, we let business carry on as usual.

#18 The Law of Rest

Before I addressed such a heavy situation, I took a moment to pause, reflect and pray.

If you do not take a moment to rest, you wind up making decisions that undo all of the time you saved by avoiding it. Not resting doesn't show ambition. It shows foolishness. As you read toward the beginning of this book, hard work is most certainly an important law of prosperity. We should not be lazy.

But the opposite extreme is just as harmful. Your mind needs rest. Your body needs sleep. Your Spirit needs prayer and the Word.

"It is useless for you to work so hard from early morning until late at night, anxiously working for food to eat; for God gives rest to his loved ones."

~ Psalm 127:2

If you will properly schedule rest into your daily agenda, you will be amazed at how much better your mind and body perform. Tired people make mistakes, have trouble thinking with clarity, fall into temptation and lack focus. I take time to golf quite often. I go see movies, and I love to travel with my wife. I rest regularly.

Don't let guilt rob you of rest.

Are you so desperate to acquire success that you forget to rest? Does blind ambition rob you of the rest that you need to prosper? Does guilt speak insults into your mind whenever you try to rest? Break free from breakdown. Rest!

The Law of Rest: Rested people prosper.

So I rested before addressing the office manager.

The office manager had no idea that he was already caught. Over that grueling period of three weeks, he and Paulie even carried out routine conversations about the company and various other casual topics. Knowing that we had no other candidate who could take the office manager's job, Paulie learned as much as he could about the office manager position. Paulie was preparing to take that position, even though he didn't really want to do it.

And then it came time to address it. I was calmer and more spiritually prepared to confront the issue. I called the head of HR –

Pastor Johnny Dorris. All of us gathered into one of the offices at Pimentel Communications. We anticipated a fleshly and even possibly aggressive response from the office manager. The moments leading up to the confrontation were tense.

When the office manager walked in to sit down for the meeting, he was very surprised to see everyone in one room: me, Paulie and Johnny Dorris. By the look on his face, we knew he was rattled, though not completely sure of why we were gathered. His jaw only slightly dropped and his eyes widened.

I began to speak, "After reviewing the payroll books, I noticed that your pay is different. What do you have to say about that?" He paused for a moment. His first words were almost dismissive, "Well, you have always told me to pay myself according to what I think I'm worth."

Knowing that to be false, I retorted firmly, "No, I have never said that." To be honest, at that point, I was just expecting this guy to give us a runaround of both excuses and lies. However, after I rejected his first excuse, he made an immediate admission. He spoke stoically, "You know what. You're right. I've made a huge mistake, and I'll pay it all back."

And before my very eyes, I saw a man breaking. The color drained from his face, and I watched him become undone and emotionally destroyed. Everything that he had worked for was potentially about to be lost. Not only did he owe a debt. He broke the law. His educational credentials would forever be overshadowed by the criminal marks on his record.

Then, something supernatural happened.

But, in that very moment, the gentle presence of the Holy Spirit descended on that room. It was as if a cloud had filled the atmosphere. It was so heavy that Paulie, who is not at all emotional, had to get up and leave to prevent himself from crying. He went to cry in the warehouse. He was even laughing at himself thinking, "Why am I crying? I don't care about this guy. He wronged us!" I'm telling you, there was a visible cloud there. It was like a fog or a mist. We all began to choke up.

But that's the work that God chose to do in that moment. We could have taken that office manager to court. We could have prosecuted him. We could have taken steps to ensure that he felt the lifelong sting of his mistakes.

But the anger that we carried for the man who had wronged us turned into divine compassion. The man who had stolen more than $25,000 from us was given his final paycheck, a paycheck he did not deserve. Not only that, but he was also forgiven of the crime he had committed against us – we chose not to press charges. And his $25,000 debt was canceled.

Had we chosen to take action against him, his career in finance would have been over. Basically, this man's life (as he knew it) was spared. How could you ever get another accounting job with a financial crime on your resume?

He didn't even want to take his paycheck. But knowing that he had no money after that point, I insisted on it. I'm telling you, it was a God thing. So, after signing a few documents and legal agreements, he left having received the mercy of God. And there was a position to fill.

As Paulie remarked, "Not only did my dad not get even with him, but he helped him and forgave him. He went in the totally opposite direction."

To this day, we have no hard feelings toward the man.

#19 The Law of Mercy

Those who are merciful are prospered of God. God looks favorably on those who show mercy. This isn't to say that you should then be a pushover. This just means that you must demonstrate your Christianity, even in a cutthroat world. Specifically, as it pertains to money, there is an old saying: when you borrow money, write it in stone. When you loan money, write it in sand. And never loan money that you can't afford to give away.

Though I seek to be wise with my resources, there have been those who have borrowed from me without ever repaying. Even worse, there have been those who have blatantly ripped me off. But I forgive and aim to become wiser with my resources. And, honestly, I believe that God has used such hurtful circumstances to test me and shape me. Besides, God is ultimately the one who guarantees my loans of compassion.

"Whoever is generous to the poor lends to the Lord, and he will repay him for his deed."
~ Proverbs 19:17

In fact, I dare say that it's almost better when man doesn't repay, because then God gets involved.

The Law of Mercy: God repays what borrowers cannot.

Strangely, I think that God used that man who ripped me off. I think it was always meant to be for Paulie to run the business with me. It was God-ordained. To be honest, I believe that my son has a double portion of the business anointing that's on my life.

Remember that my mindset is an old school one. Recall the way I was raised. Well, Paulie has a different mindset, a mind that thinks much bigger than I do. Don't get me wrong. Paulie made mistakes. I must have fired him over a dozen times. And he and I worked through the relationship dynamics of a father and a son running a company.

But when he took over the office, business began to boom. We got much larger contracts for much larger projects – universities, hospitals, computer companies and more. Projects just seemed to come our way.

But I am just a man. Even at the height of blessing, God had to work with my own doubts and reservations. Never have I had to have a salesman. Projects just come.

And, during certain times, I like to forecast and plan. And, in those times, I don't always see how any more work will come our way – it just doesn't always seem possible. But God always provides.

In fact, there was one time in particular where I could see that we were just about to run out of work. So I began to plan a search for a salesman. In fact, I even interviewed several people who were interested in the job. While considering the new hire, I was rebuked by the Holy Spirit. He was straight to the point, "Let me remind you. This is My company, not yours. You dedicated it to Me. *I am your Salesman.*"

I'm sure that one day God will direct me to hire a sales staff. But for the time being, whenever I have trouble seeing how work will come our way, I just go to God and remind Him of His promises.

Now, our company does millions of dollars worth of business every single year. I say this so that you can become inspired. When hearing about the success of others, you can choose to become one of two things.

Become jealous…
Or…
Become inspired.

My wife and I fund the Kingdom. We donate 40-50% of our income towards the gospel. We give away hundreds of thousands of dollars to mission projects, ministries and churches. We fund church buildings and church remodels. We even support Christian television. Lori and I are the executive producers of Encounter TV with David Diga Hernandez.

And now you know the story behind such prosperity. But, even during a season of great blessing, my faith was tested like it had never been before.

Chapter 7
Something is Coming

The test came in a way I least expected – as tests often do. But I can't say that I was blindsided. Because I remained closely dependent upon God, even during a season of abundance, I was able to sense His leading, though it was subtle. I had an odd sense of anticipation. But, as far as I was able to tell, everything was normal. The business was doing well. My family wasn't experiencing any strain. And even the church was in a fruitful season. Even still, a persistent sense of foreboding loomed over me like an eager vulture circling its prey.

#20 The Law of Mastery

What I was about to face would challenge me in every possible way. Looking back, I don't know what I would have done if I didn't have the Lord. What if I, like some, were to trade masters?

What if money had become my master?

Of all the laws of prosperity, this one deserves your most attention, because it's so easy to break. Master money. Don't let it master you. How do you know when you've been mastered by money? When you aim to earn it for its own sake.

"Those who love money will never have enough. How meaningless to think that wealth brings true happiness!"
~ Ecclesiastes 5:10

You know money is your master when you…

…think of it more than you think of God
…desire it more than you desire God
…trust it more than you trust God

"No one can serve two masters. For you will hate one and love the other; you will be devoted to one and despise the other. You cannot serve both God and money."

~ Matthew 6:24

God is so powerful that even His servants become masters of money. Don't become ruled by what is not royalty. Don't become mastered by what is rightfully your servant.

Do you desire money more than you desire God? Does your giving toward the gospel decrease in percentage as your finances increase in amount? Does your giving toward the gospel decrease in percentage as your finances decrease in amount? Make money your slave before it enslaves you. Send it where it doesn't want to go.

The Law of Mastery: Make money your slave before it enslaves you.

In April of 2009, God started to deal with me firstly in my schedule. My much traveling became some traveling, and then my some traveling became no traveling. The Lord told me to hold off on the traveling and to clear my schedule. So I refused to book any more trips and even canceled previously made travel plans. From July 2009 to 2010, my calendar was cleared. Only a missionary trip to South Africa remained on my schedule for the month of May.

Because of all the sudden cancellations I made, some people thought that I was angry with them.

But that wasn't all that changed. Even my eating habits began to change. I became health conscious. I started to exercise routinely. I was a treadmill maniac. I would even leave my stats on the machine for Lori to see. As a result of the dietary changes and working out, I lost 40 pounds.

And even my interests began to change. I started to become more globally minded, turning my attention to politics and world events. I began to pay attention to the political climate of the nation and economic trends. It was unlike me to be aware of such things.

The changes in me were so drastic that Johnny Dorris thought that I was having an affair and confronted me with his concern. I explained that it wasn't an affair, but that was all I could tell him. Not even I could understand all of those changes.

Preparing for my trip to Africa, I underwent the standard medical examinations necessary to take the trip. I also received my shots to help protect me against H1N1, Malaria and such. And to top it off, I was given a PSA test blood – it's basically a blood test that measures the amount of a certain protein being produced by the prostate. You don't want your PSA count to be too high.

A week passed after the testing, and the hospital staff contacted me on the phone. It was then that I was informed of an irregularity in my blood – they thought they saw *something* in my blood.

Frightened, I began to call certain people and enlisted their prayers. Mind you, I only called a few people. Not everyone. And, of course, I also told my church and family.

After receiving consultation from my urologist, I was retested five more times over a period of 5 long months. Finally, my urologist recommended that I have a biopsy done on my prostate.

My dad had died of prostate cancer, so I was very anxious about the idea. I really didn't want to have the biopsy done, because I honestly didn't want to know the results. I was afraid to know the results.

But my sister-in-law, a nurse practitioner, after going through my medical records with me, strongly urged me to have the biopsy done. Of course, I had my concerns, "I don't want them messing around there. They could ruin something."

Regardless of my resistance to the idea, my sister-in-law convinced me. I had the biopsy done.

After a very long week, the results of the biopsy were in. All of the testing and medical back-and-forth made me realize why I had to have my schedule cleared – I was able to make consistent and time-sensitive appointments.

Once the results were in, I was notified of their arrival by phone. The earliest appointment they had available was for the next day in the afternoon. To me, the sooner the better. The wait was causing an obnoxious apprehension to harass my mind. Though I was filled with faith, the whole experience was beginning to take a toll on my emotions. I just wanted to receive good news. I went into the situation declaring, by faith, that I was going to receive a good medical report.

Though my appointment was scheduled for the afternoon, someone else canceled their early morning slot. So I was given the option to go in earlier. Obviously, I took the opportunity. I just wanted to get it over with.

I arrived at the doctor's office and was seated by a member of the doctor's staff. I waited for a few minutes, and then my doctor stepped into the room. She had some files in her hand. She stared down at them as she walked over to me. My heart was beating very fast.

But there was no build up, no preparation for what she told me. As she walked in, she very casually, without emotion, with no hesitation, told me, "You have first stage cancer. What do you want to do?" Her tone was normal, as if she were telling me the weather or updating me on a score.

I tried to comprehend her words, but I was in shock. At first my mind tried to deny what I was told. Then I tried to wrap my thoughts around the question, "What do you want to do?" But I couldn't wrap my mind around that question, because I still could not believe what I was being told. I wasn't given time to react or process the reality.

I was inundated with charts, treatment methods, percentages and probabilities. I was feeling the pressure to express an interest in one of the treatment methods. However, I wasn't even sure if I had yet accepted the diagnosis. Was there a mistake? Were they certain that I had cancer? I had many questions but not the presence of mind to ask them. Sensing an unfamiliar feeling of helplessness and surprised at my own reaction, I thought to myself, "I wish Lori was here. I should have brought my wife."

Eventually, I stepped outside of the little room, and it was as if I left an entire world behind. Still struggling to cope with my new reality, I had fallen asleep to my old life and was now experiencing a nightmare. I wanted nothing more than to wake up and have my old reality come rushing back to me.

I felt my phone pulsing on my leg. The vibration snapped me out of the haze for a few seconds. It was a missed called from Paulie. By impulse, I called him back. But I hadn't even thought of what to say to him. What was I to tell him? I could hear the ringing in my ear, but I wasn't sure of what to say. It was all happening so fast. Paulie answered. Words were speeding passed my mind, and I was struggling to choose the ones best suited for the moment. All I could manage to say was, "Hi, Paulie". In that instant, a fresh wave of overwhelming emotion rushed over me. I began to cry.

I moved my mouth but couldn't break any words beyond the barrier of my tearful state. Finding just a few seconds of breaking composure, I managed to stammer, "I have cancer. Meet me at the house. We have to tell mom."

Paulie and I met at my house where Lori was waiting. She could see us approaching the front door, but she had no idea that my appointment was changed to an earlier time. As far as she knew, I wasn't to receive my test results until later that afternoon.

So she had hoped that I was joking when she opened the door to my straightforward and startling announcement: "I have cancer."

Her response broke me inside. She looked at me and asserted, "No, you don't." She wanted to believe her own words. So did I. But I had to reiterate, "Really. I have cancer." Lori glanced over at Paulie and realized that he was there for a reason. She looked back over at me and embraced me. All we could do was cry. I spoke words of hopeful resolve, "We're going to beat this."

I made phone calls to my kids. That was tough.

That was a tough Tuesday.

But we had church service on Wednesday night, and I was not going to miss it. My church was also awaiting the results of the biopsy. I wasted no time. Immediately after worship, I announced that I had cancer. From the congregation, I heard a gasp, then a short silence, followed by sporadic crying. I cried, and the church cried with me.

But when we were done crying, I made a proclamation: "We've cried. Now there's no more crying. There's just faith."

Many were shocked, but, if I am being honest with you and myself, I knew I had it. After all, I figured that God had to be preparing me for something. In fact, two ladies gently approached me after the service and told me that they too had known, because they noticed the changes and my cleared schedule.

I live in obedience to God. I am a citizen of His kingdom and His son. My job is to trust and obey. And God takes it from there. When I was diagnosed with cancer, I thought of when Paul the apostle was bitten by a viper (**Acts 28:1-6**). Though others considered him as good as dead, he simply shook it off. I did the same. I just shook it off. That Paul should have died, and this Paul should have died. But God is able to do above and beyond what we can think.

Taking the situation from a position of faith, I was empowered throughout the entirety of the struggle. I was in a storm, but the storm was never inside of me. It was with that attitude that I faced what was ahead.

I was given the option to have my prostate removed or to just go through radiation – or both. With only radiation, the cancer was likely to come back within 5 years. So I chose both radiation treatment and removal. I went at it with full assault.

#21 The Law of Practicality

My choosing to take medical treatment wasn't because of a lack of faith in God. In fact, everything we do should cooperate with God's will. We must do the difficult, while God does the impossible.

Is sickness God's will? No, it is not. So I did everything in my natural ability to align myself with God's will, and then I left the supernatural to Him. Though we walk by faith, we must keep our sense of practicality.

Some are unrealistic in their expectations of blessings. People sow $5 in an offering one time and then expect God to get them out of debt. They tithe for three months and expect years of poor financial planning to just vanish. We need to plan, budget, invest, research, pay our bills and work a job. From there, God progressively increases us.

In believing for the supernatural, we cannot forget to do the practical.

The Law of Practicality: Believing for the supernatural doesn't mean that we should stop doing the practical.

Over the next three months, I was given a test a month. A peculiar thing was that I was receiving treatment and testing in the very same hospital for which my company provided the fiber optics. The machines ran on cables that my company installed. In fact, one of the medical personnel, while preparing me for a test, commented to me, "Let's see if your wiring works for you, Mr. Pimentel."

After those three trying months, having received radiation treatment and having undergone a procedure to have my prostate removed, I was given an update. The update wasn't the best, and it wasn't the worst.

The cancer had breached the wall of my prostate, so the removal didn't get all of the cancer. But neither had the cancer entered my bones or blood. The doctors could see it and were confident that they could remove it.

Over the next seven weeks, radiation was targeted at my cancer. The radiation machine, a six million dollar piece of equipment, run by ten high-tech computers, was positioned on the other side of a led wall. On that wall was a sign that simply read, "Believe." I took it as a literal sign from God.

And as I was undergoing those radiation treatments, my employees were working down the hall installing more communication cabling. The treatments were given at two-minute intervals, Monday through Friday, for seven weeks.

And each time, I would be worshipping and praying in tongues while undergoing the treatment. I was told that I would lose my hair, bleed internally, become nauseous, receive burn marks on my skin and develop consistent fatigue.

I did experience fatigue but very little. I had none of the other symptoms. I still worked and golfed regularly. I even continued to preach and attend church. And, actually, my hair even came out thicker than before. Because of my healthy appearance, energy level and uplifted demeanor, the other patients couldn't believe that I was undergoing the same treatment as them. I would explain to them, "I'm connected to the Lord, the guy upstairs."

But the experience was changing me for the better. I became more sensitive and compassionate. I was given a new and greater appreciation of life. That's no cliché – it really does happen.

Sure I had my moments of weakness. But in every moment of weakness, I would "randomly" receive a call from someone who would encourage me and pray with me. Other than God, my family and church family helped to see me through the darkness of that period.

Today, I am cancer free.

My life isn't over. And I'm still going strong. As I continue upon this exhilarating journey of faith, I hold within my heart the certainty of God's Word, the power of the Holy Spirit and the love of Jesus. Though far from complete, I've been through too much to ever become unconvinced of this liberating truth: God's not broke.

21 Laws of Prosperity

#1 The Law of Work: Prosperity is on purpose.

#2 The Law of Covenant: God can be approached with requests and deals.

#3 The Law of Firsts: God prospers those who give their first and best to Him.

#4 The Law of Knowledge: The more you know the further you go.

#5 The Law of Honor and Humility: Humility demonstrated through honor opens doors that lead to your destiny.

#6 The Law of Faith: Faith reveals, step by step, the progressive path to prosperity.

#7 The Law of Obedience: Obedience produces perfect position.

#8 The Law of Greatness: A life of greatness is created in the daily acts of faithfulness.

#9 The Law of Persistence: If you keep going, you will eventually reach your destination – no exceptions.

#10 The Law of Declaration: Words create atmospheres and influence reality.

#11 The Law of Honesty: If a man is not honest, he can never be prosperous.

#12 The Law of the Word: If prosperity is a destination then the Bible is the map.

#13 The Law of Wisdom: Prosperity is given in proportion to wisdom.

#14 The Law of Reciprocity: God gives returns on your Heavenly investments.

#15 The Law of Good Company: Good company accelerates your pace toward prosperity, and bad company does the opposite.

#16 The Law of Generosity: The generous will prosper.

#17 The Law of Contentment: Appreciating what you have shows God that you can handle more.

#18 The Law of Rest: Rested people prosper.

#19 The Law of Mercy: God repays what borrowers cannot.

#20 The Law of Mastery: Make money your slave before it enslaves you.

#21 The Law of Practicality: Believing for the supernatural doesn't mean that we should stop doing the practical.